SELECT TITLES BY M.L. HUMP

WORD ESSENTIALS 2019

Word 2019 Beginner

Word 2019 Intermediate

POWERPOINT ESSENTIALS 2019

PowerPoint 2019 Beginner

PowerPoint 2019 Intermediate

EXCEL ESSENTIALS 2019

Excel 2019 Beginner

Excel 2019 Intermediate

Excel 2019 Formulas & Functions

Excel 2019 Formulas and Functions Study Guide

ACCESS ESSENTIALS 2019

Access 2019 Beginner

Access 2019 Intermediate

CONTENTS

Word 2019 Beginner

WORD ESSENTIALS 2019 BOOK 1

M.L. HUMPHREY

CONTENTS

Introduction

The purpose of this guide is to introduce you to the basics of using Microsoft Word 2019. While there are a number of other word processing programs out there, Word is still the gold-standard go-to program in use in large portions of the corporate world, so if you're going to be involved in a white collar job (and even some blue collar jobs), being familiar with Word will be a significant advantage for you. And essential for many jobs. (The days of having an assistant who could do those things for you are gone.)

Word at its most basic is incredibly simple to use. You open a new file, type in your text, save, and done.

But chances are you'll want control over the appearance of what you type. Maybe you need to use a different font or font size. Maybe you want to indent your paragraphs. Or include a bulleted or numbered list.

That's where this guide comes in. First I will walk you through the absolute basics (open, save, delete) but then most of this guide will be focused on what to do with your text once it's been typed into your document.

Having said that I'm not going to cover everything you can do in Word. The goal of this guide is to get you up to speed and comfortable with what you'll need for probably 98% of what you'll use Word for on a daily basis.

Some of the exceptions to that are if you're working in an environment where you need to use track changes with a group of users or you need to create something like tables or complex multilevel lists. Those are more advanced topics that are covered in *Word 2019 Intermediate*.

The goal here is to give you a solid foundation that you can work from.

As noted in the title and above, this book is written using Word 2019. I previously wrote a book, *Word for Beginners*, that was written using Word 2013 and was written to be generic enough that any user of Word could learn the basics from it. But this guide is written specifically for Word 2019, so I'm not going to mention what wasn't possible in older version of Word, for example.

As a beginner it probably won't matter. Where it becomes more relevant is at the intermediate level. But just so you know. The focus in this guide is Word 2019.

Alright then. Let's get started with some basic terminology.

Basic Terminology

Before we get started, I want to make sure that we're on the same page in terms of terminology.

Tab

I refer to the menu choices at the top of the screen (File, Home, Insert, Design, Layout, References, Mailings, Review, View, and Help) as tabs. If you click on one you'll see that the way it's highlighted sort of looks like an old-time filing system like below with the Home tab.

Each tab you select will show you different options.

For example, in the image above, I have the Home tab selected and you can do various tasks such as cut/copy/paste, format paint, change the font, change the formatting of a paragraph, apply a style to your text, find/replace words in your document, or select the text in your document. Other tabs give other options.

Click

If I tell you to click on something, that means to use your mouse (or trackpad) to move the arrow on the screen over to a specific location and left-click or right-click on the option. (See the next definition for the difference between left-click and right-click).

If you left-click, this generally selects an item. If you right-click, this generally creates a dropdown list of options to choose from. If I don't tell you which to do, left- or right-click, then left-click.

Left-Click/Right-Click

If you look at your mouse or your trackpad, you generally have two flat buttons to press. One is on the left side, one is on the right. If I say left-click that means to press down on the button on the left. If I say right-click that means press down on the button on the right.

Not all track pads have left- and right-hand buttons. In that case, you'll basically want to press on either the bottom left-hand side of the track pad or the bottom right-hand side of the trackpad. Since you're working blind it may take a little trial and error to get the option you want.

Select or Highlight

If I tell you to select text, that means to left-click at the end of the text you want to select, hold that left-click, and move your cursor to the other end of the text.

Another option is to use the Shift key. Go to one end of the text you want to select. Hold down the shift key and use the arrow keys to move to the other end of the text. If you arrow up or down, that will select an entire row at a time.

With both methods, which side of the text you start on doesn't matter. You can start at the end and go to the beginning or start at the beginning and go to the end. Just be sure to start at one end or the other. You cannot start in the middle

The text you've selected will then be highlighted in gray. Like the words "sample text" in this image:

This is sample text so you can see what I'm talking about.

If you need to select text that isn't touching you can do this by selecting your first section of text and then holding down the Ctrl key and selecting your second section of text using your mouse. (You can't arrow to the second section of text or you'll lose your already selected text.)

Dropdown Menu

If you right-click in a Word document, you will see what I'm going to refer to as a dropdown menu. (Sometimes it will actually drop upward if you're towards the bottom of the document.)

A dropdown menu provides you a list of choices to select from.

There are also dropdown menus available for some of the options listed under the tabs at the top of the screen.

For example, if you go to the Paragraph section of the Home tab, you will see arrows next to the options for bulleted lists, numbered lists, multi-level lists, line and paragraph spacing, shading, and borders.

Dropdown Arrows

If you click on any of those arrows you'll see a list of additional choices.

Expansion Arrows

I don't know the official word for these, but you'll also notice at the bottom right corner of most of the sections in each tab that there are little arrows. If you hold your mouse over the arrow you will see a brief description of what clicking on the expansion arrow will do like below with Paragraph Settings.

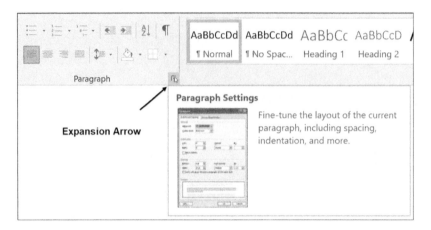

In general, clicking on that arrow will then open a dialogue box although sometimes a task pane will open instead.

Dialogue Box

Dialogue boxes, such as this one for Find and Replace, are pop-up boxes that cover specialized settings.

As just mentioned, if you click on an expansion arrow, it will often open a dialogue box that contains more choices than are visible in that section.

When you right-click in a Word document and choose Font, Paragraph, or Hyperlink from the dropdown menu that also opens a dialogue box

Some of the menu options will do so as well. For example, clicking on Replace in the Editing section of the Home tab will bring up the Find and Replace dialogue box. (As will using Ctrl + H, which is a control shortcut. We'll define those momentarily.)

Dialogue boxes often allow the most granular level of control over an option so if you can't find what you want in the menu section tabs at the top, try opening the relevant dialogue box.

Also, be aware that if you have more than one Word document open and open a dialogue box in one of those documents, you may not be able to move to the other documents you have open until you close the dialogue box.

Task Pane

Sometimes instead of opening a dialogue box, Excel will open what I refer to as a task pane. These are separate panes that appear to the right, left, or bottom of your main workspace. (As opposed to a dialogue box which generally appears as a separate item on top of your workspace.)

I believe the Navigation pane is open on the left-hand side by default for any new document for new users of Word. It will show headings if you use those in your document and is also the default location if you try to use Find in your document.

Task panes can be closed by clicking on the X in the top right corner. If you close the Navigation pane and want it back, Ctrl + F, which is for Find, will open it again.

Clicking on the expansion arrow for the Clipboard section of the Home tab also opens a task pane.

Scroll Bar

This is more useful in Excel than in Word, but on the right-hand side of the screen and sometimes at the bottom of the screen you may see a scroll bar which will allow you to see the rest of your document if it's too large or too long to be fully visible on the screen.

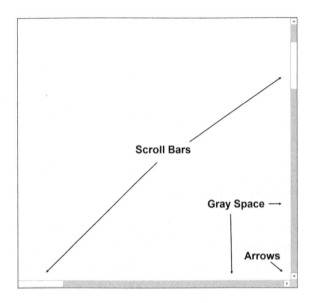

You can click in the gray space around the bar to move up or down a small amount. Or you can left-click on the bar, hold the left-click, and drag the bar to move through the document more quickly.

You can also use the arrows at the ends to move through your document.

The scroll bar isn't always visible in Word. If you don't see it, move your mouse over to the side of the screen and it should appear.

Also, by default you normally won't see a scroll bar at the bottom of the screen, but it is possible to see one, usually when you have your document or screen zoomed in.

Arrow

If I ever tell you to arrow to the left or right or up or down, that just means use your arrow keys. This will move your cursor to the left one space, to the right one space, up one line, or down one line. If you're at the end of a line and arrow to the right, it will take you to the beginning of the next line. If you're at the beginning of a line and arrow to the left, it will take you to the end of the last line.

Cursor

There are two possible meanings for cursor. One is the one I just used. In your Word document, you will see that there is a blinking line. This indicates where you are in the document. If you type text, each letter will appear where the cursor was at the time you typed it. The cursor will move (at least in the U.S. and I'd assume most European versions) to the right as you type. This version of the cursor should be visible at all times unless you have text selected.

The other type of cursor is the one that's tied to the movement of your mouse or trackpad. When you're typing, it will not be visible. But stop typing and move your mouse or trackpad, and you'll see it.

If the cursor is positioned over your text, it will look somewhat like a tall skinny capital I. If you move it up to the menu options or off to the sides, it becomes a white arrow. (Except for when you position it over any option under the tabs that can be typed in such as Font Size or Font where it will once again look like a skinny capital I.)

Usually I won't refer to your cursor, I'll just say, "click" or "select" or whatever action you need to take with it. Moving the cursor to that location will be implied.

I may also sometimes refer to this as moving your mouse or holding your mouse over something instead of moving your cursor or holding your cursor over an item.

Quick Access Toolbar

In the very top left corner of Word is something called the Quick Access Toolbar. By default it contains icons that let you save, undo, and redo. Bur you can customize your options for tasks that you use often by clicking on that arrow at the end and choosing from the dropdown menu it will bring up.

For example, I will usually customize mine to include inserting section breaks because those are listed on a different tab than the text formatting options I also need to be using at the same time. This saves me having to move back and forth between the two.

Control Shortcuts

What I refer to as control shortcuts are easy and quick ways to complete common tasks by using the Ctrl key paired with, generally, a letter.

I mentioned the Find control shortcut, Ctrl + F, above as well as the Replace shortcut, Ctrl + H. So, for example, by typing Ctrl and the letter H at the same time you can open the Replace dialogue box that allows you to replace text in your document with different text.

When I refer to a control shortcut, I write the letter as a capital letter, but you don't actually have to use the capitalized version of the letter. It just means hold down the control key and that letter at the same time.

There is a list of control shortcuts at the back of this book. It is not a comprehensive list, but I highly recommend that you memorize the ones that are there. They will save you a tremendous amount of time over the years.

Absolute Basics

Before we do anything else, there are a few absolute basics that we should cover.

Starting a New Word File

To start a brand new Word file, click on Word from your applications menu or, if you have one, the shortcut on your computer's taskbar. Either choice will bring up a welcome screen with a list of various options or templates, including the first one which is for a "Blank document". Ninety-nine percent of the time that's the one you'll want. To use it, left-click on the image.

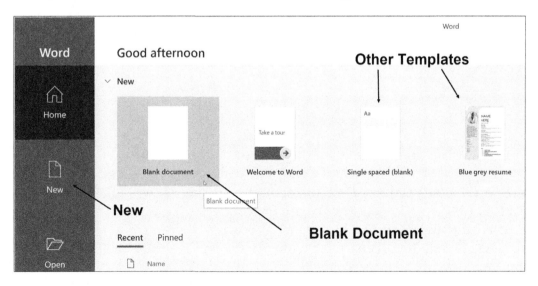

If you're already in Word and want to start a new Word file, go to the File tab and choose New from the left-hand menu. It will again show various choices. This time the Blank Document choice will be at the top and other templates will be shown below.

You can also the control shortcut Ctrl +N while in an existing document and a new blank document will immediately open.

Opening an Existing Word File

To open an existing Word file you can either go to the folder where the file is saved and double-click on the file name. Or, if the file is one you used recently, you can instead open Word and choose the file from the list of Recent documents. (If it's a file you've pinned even if it hasn't been used recently, you can still choose it from the list of Pinned documents.)

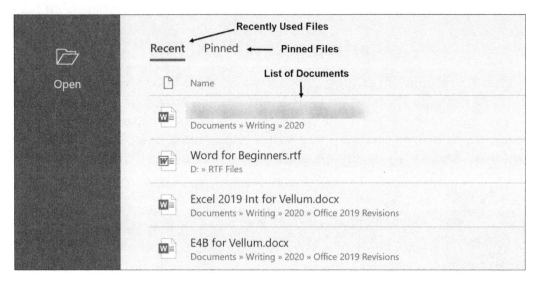

If you already have a Word file open, you can also go to the File tab and choose any recently used document from the Recent documents list.

To choose a file from within Word, left-click on it once, and it will open as long as you haven't renamed the file or moved it since it was last opened.

(In that case, you'll need to navigate to where the file is saved and open it that way, either through Word or outside of Word.)

To navigate to a file, click on Open from the sidebar, then click on the location where the document is stored.

If you use OneDrive click on that. I don't, so I click on Browse to open a standard Windows dialogue box. Mine defaults to the Documents folder on This PC. I can then navigate through my folders or shortcuts from there and click on the file I need.

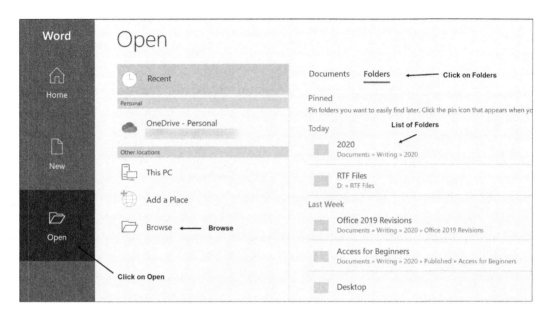

You can also click on Folders on the right-hand side to display a list of folders that contain files you've recently used. Click on one of the folder names to bring up a list of the files and folders that are in that folder.

It will show the files and folders within the Word workspace. Only documents that can be opened in Word will be listed.

Saving a Word File

If you want to keep the changes you made to a document, you need to save it. To do so quickly, you can use Ctrl + S or click on the small image of a floppy disk in the Quick Access Toolbar in the top left corner of the screen above File.

For a document you've already saved, that will overwrite the prior version of the document with the current version while keeping the file name, file type, and file location the same.

If you try to save a file that has never been saved before, Word will automatically default to the Save As option and open a Save This File dialogue box which asks for the file name you want to use and a location to save the file in.

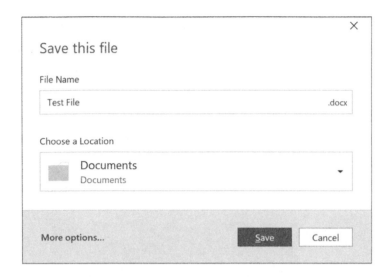

Type your file name into the box for File Name, choose your location from the Choose a Location dropdown, and then click Save.

The default file type with this option is .docx which should be fine for most purposes.

If you are working with someone who has a version of Word that dates prior to 2007, you'll need to save the file as a .doc file. To do so, click on the More Options choice at the bottom of the dialogue box.

This will take you to the Save As option on the File tab screen. From there you can double-click on a location to save your file and this will open a Save As dialogue box which lets you choose your file type as well.

Even for an existing document there will still be times when you need to use the Save As option to change the location of a file, the name of a file, or the file type.

(With respect to file type, I often need to save a .doc file as a .pdf file or a .docx file or to save a .docx file as a .doc file, for example.)

You can reach the Save As option while working with an existing file by clicking on the File tab and then the Save As option on the left-hand side.

From there double-click on your location and make whatever necessary changes you need to make in the dialogue box that opens. (If the location is not listed, you can get the dialogue box to open and then navigate to your preferred location using the left-hand side options.)

To rename a file, it's actually best to close the file and then go to where the file is currently saved and rename it that way rather than using the Save As option within Word.

This is because if you use Save As, Word will keep the original version of the file with the old name as well as create a version with the new name. That's great when you want version control, but not when you just wanted to rename your file and now can't remember which version is the most current one.

(This is a good opportunity to point out that using something like YYYYMMDD or V1, V2, etc. in your file names can really help with keeping version control. If I have a file named Great Report 20201220 and one named Great Report 20201101, I can easily tell which is the most current version. They will also sort in order if you use YYYYMMDD format for the dates in the file name and place the date in the exact same spot in the name each time.)

Renaming a Word File

As discussed above, you can use Save As to give an existing file a new name, but that approach will leave you with two versions of the file, one with the old name and one with the new name. If you just want to change the name of the existing file, close it and then navigate to where you've saved it.

Click on the file name once to select it, click on it a second time to highlight the name, and then type in the new name you want to use, replacing the old one.

If you rename the file this way outside of Word, there will only be one version of the file left, the one with the new name you wanted.

Just be aware that if you rename a file by navigating to where it's located and changing the name that you then won't be able to access the file from the Recent Workbooks listing under Open file, since that listing will still list the old name which no longer exists.

(This actually applies for any file that is moved, renamed, or in a location that is no longer available. If you look at that file listing above, my file Word for Beginners was in a location D: which was a removable thumb drive. I don't have that thumb drive attached to my computer at the moment, so if I tried to click on that file name right now I would see an error telling me that the directory name isn't valid. I personally run into this issue more with moved files than I do with renamed ones, but it's something to be aware of.)

Deleting a Word File

You can't delete a Word file from within Word. You need to close the file you want to delete and then navigate to where the file is stored and delete the file there without opening it. Once you've located the file, click on the file name. (Only enough to select it. Make sure you haven't double-clicked and highlighted the name which will delete the file name but not the file.) Next, choose Delete from the menu at the top of the screen, or right-click and choose Delete from the dropdown menu.

Closing a Word File

To close a Word file click on the X in the top right corner. You can also go to File and then choose Close which will keep Word open if that was your last Word file.

(You can also use Ctrl + W, but I never have. That also closes the file but leaves Word open.)

If no changes were made to the document since you saved it last, the document will just close.

If changes have been made, Word will ask you if you want to save those changes. Your choices are to Save, Don't Save, or Cancel. For a brand new document you need to provide a file name and choose a location. For an existing one, Word will assume the file name and location are going to stay the same.

If you cancel, the document remains open. If you save, it will overwrite the prior version of the document with any changes you've made. If you choose don't save, then the version of the document that remains will be the one that existed last time you saved. Or, in the case of a new document, that document will be lost.

I almost always default to saving any changes. If I'm in doubt about whether I'd be overwriting something important, I cancel and choose to Save As and save the current file as a later version of the document just in case (e.g., Great Book v2).

If right before you closed the document you copied an image or a large block of text, you may also see a dialogue box asking if you want to keep that image or text on the clipboard to paste elsewhere Usually the answer for me is no, but if you had planned on pasting that image or text somewhere else and hadn't yet done so, you can say to keep it on the clipboard.

Basic Tasks

At its most basic, adding text into a Word document is incredibly simple. Just open a new blank document and start typing. When you're done, save the document.

But you probably want to do more with your text than that.

We'll cover all the formatting, which is the majority of what you'll want to do, in the next section. First, I want to cover a few basic tasks in Word that will make your life easier as you enter your text and then edit it.

Undo

Undo lets you take the last thing (or few things) you did, and undo it. That means you don't have to be afraid to try something that you're not sure will work, because you can always reverse it.

To undo something, simply type Ctrl + Z. If you did a few things you didn't like you can keep typing Ctrl + Z until they're all gone.

Your other option is to use the undo arrow in the Quick Access Toolbar. It's the left-pointing arrow and will only be an option to click on when there's something that can be undone.

When there are multiple actions that can be undone the Quick Access Toolbar option will also include a dropdown arrow. You can click on it to see a full listing of what actions can be undone.

Keep in mind that Word undoes things in order. So if you highlighted text, bolded that text, and then underlined it and you want to undo the highlight, you'll have to undo the bolding and underline as well.

You can't pick and choose.

When there are multiple steps to undo the Quick Access Toolbar option is the better choice because you can simply choose the last item on the list that you wanted to undo and it as well as all of the actions that were taken after it will be undone.

Redo

If you take it too far and undo too much and want something back, then you can choose to redo. That's done by typing Ctrl + Y.

There is also a Redo option on the Quick Access Toolbar. It's the right-pointing arrow.

It works much like the Undo option since it's only available when there is something that can be redone, but it will only redo one action at a time. So in my example above where I could undo three actions at once, to put them back in place I had to do each one individually.

Delete

Another basic task you need to master is how to delete text. There are a few ways to do this. If you're trying to delete something that you just typed, use the backspace key to delete the letters one at a time.

You can also click into your text to place the cursor next to the text you want to delete and then use the backspace or delete keys depending on where the cursor is relative to the text you're trying to delete.

If your cursor is on the left-hand side of text, use the delete key. If it's on the right-hand side, use the backspace key. (And if you get it wrong, remember that you have Ctrl + Z to undo what you just did.)

If you want to delete a large chunk of text at one time, select the text first and then use the delete OR backspace key.

Select All

The other basic task that you should know about before we start talking formatting is how to select all of the text in your document.

Select All is very useful for applying a format to your entire document or for copying text from one document to another or another program.

I tend to write in the default font that Word uses and then change the font once I'm done, for example.

The easiest way to select all of your text is to use Ctrl + A. You can also go to the Editing section of the Home tab, click on the arrow next to Select, and choose Select All from the dropdown menu.

I have also added Select All as one of my Quick Access Toolbar options in the past.

If you ever choose all of the text in a document and then decide you didn't want to, just click somewhere in the document and the selection will go away. (You can also arrow up or down, but that will take you to the top or the bottom of the document and you may not want that.)

Copying, Cutting, and Pasting

Copy and Cut are similar. They're both a way to move text from one location to another. Copy leaves the text where it was and creates a copy of that text to move to the new location. Cut removes the text from where it was and puts the text on a "clipboard" (that's usually not visible to you) for movement to a new location.

Paste is how you tell Word where that new location is regardless of whether you copied or cut the text.

The first step in copying or cutting text is to select all of the text you want to move.

As discussed before, to select text you can left-click at one end of the text, hold down that left-click and move your mouse or trackpad until all of the text you want is highlighted. Or you can click at one end of the text and use the shift key and the arrow keys. Your selected text will be highlighted in gray.

Once your text is selected, to copy it type Ctrl + C or to cut it type Ctrl + X.

If you don't want to use the control shortcuts, you can also go to the Clipboard section of the Home tab and choose Copy or Cut from there. Or you can right-click and choose Copy or Cut from the dropdown menu.

I recommend using the control shortcuts, because it's the easiest and fastest option and doesn't require using your mouse or trackpad.

If you copy text, it remains visible in the location you copied it from. Behind the scenes Word has taken a copy of that text and placed it on a "clipboard" for use elsewhere.

If you cut text, the text is immediately removed from the document. It too is placed on a "clipboard" for use elsewhere. (This also means that cutting text, if you choose not to paste it elsewhere, deletes it.)

If you want to collect multiple selections of text to eventually paste elsewhere, click on the expansion arrow for the Clipboard section of the Home tab. This will open the clipboard. You can then select different sections of your document and copy or cut them and they should appear on the clipboard for your use.

(It looks like it should also work even if you don't have the clipboard open at the time you're copying or cutting multiple selections, but best practice would be to have it visible so you know that the items your are copying or cutting are being captured properly.) Here I've selected three snippets of text. Two were copied, one was cut, but there's no difference in how they appear on the clipboard.

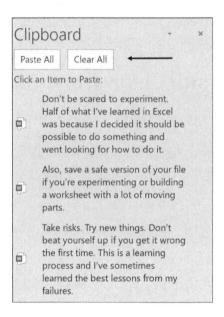

If you ever copy or cut items to your clipboard and decide you don't want them, just choose Clear All. Otherwise click on where you want to paste an individual item in your document and then click on the item in the clipboard to paste it.

The Paste All option will paste all of your copied or cut selections into that one location.

Items remain on the clipboard after they are pasted which means you can technically paste something into your document multiple times using the clipboard option.

If all you want to do is just copy or cut one thing and paste it one time, then using the paste control shortcut is going to be easier. To paste use Ctrl + V. So highlight your selection, copy (Ctrl + C) or cut (Ctrl +X) it, go to where you want to place it and click into the document, use Ctrl + V to paste it, and you're done.

Rather than use Ctrl + V to paste you can also go to the Clipboard section of the Home tab and click on Paste from there or right-click in your document and choose one of the Paste options from the dropdown menu.

The reason to use one of those options instead of just Ctrl + V is because it gives you control over the formatting of the text when you paste it, so let's talk about those options now.

Paste Options

If you use Ctrl + V to paste text, you'll be pasting not only the text you copied or cut, but its formatting as well. Usually, that's fine and you'll probably be able to use Ctrl + V ninety-five percent of the time.

(Even if you ultimately don't want to keep the formatting, there's a trick I'll show you later—using the Format Painter—that you can use to quickly correct formatting after you paste the text into its new location. All the Format Painter requires is that you have some text that's already formatted the way you want so you can copy its formatting.)

But in case you do want control over how you paste in your text, that's where the Paste Options can be used. There are four paste options: Keep Source Formatting, Merge Formatting, Picture, and Keep Text Only.

As you can see here, when you hold your cursor over each option it will tell you which option that one is. I have my cursor over the first option which is Keep Source Formatting and that description is shown directly below the option as I hold my cursor there.

The best way to figure out what each of these options does is to just experiment with them. That's what I've done below.

I took the word TEST and I formatted it in a larger font, a different font, bolded it, colored the text red, and highlighted the text in yellow. (You may not see all of that in print, but I can describe it for you.) I then copied that text and pasted it into each of my sample sentences using the different paste methods above.

The first paste option was just using Ctrl + V and that pasted the text in with all of the formatting I'd applied still in place.

TEST

Ctrl + V (Paste)

Sample **TEST** text for demonstration purposes.

Keep Source Formatting

Sample **TEST** text for demonstration purposes.

Merge Formatting

Sample **TEST** text for demonstration purposes.

Picture

Sample

TEST

text for demonstration purposes.

Keep Text Only

Sample TEST text for demonstration purposes.

The second option, Keep Formatting, also kept everything. The third option, Merge Formatting, lost the different font size, different font, font color, and highlight. But it kept the bolding.

The fourth option, Picture, actually pasted the copied text in as a picture in a picture box.

And the final option, Keep Text Only stripped way all of the formatting I'd applied, including the bolding.

Interesting, but my recommendation is to stick to Ctrl + V and use the Format Painter when and if needed.

Okay. On to text formatting. If you remember anything from what we just walked through, remember this:

Ctrl + C to copy.

Ctrl + X to cut.

Ctrl + V to paste.

Text Formatting

Now that you know how to create a file, enter the text you want, and save your work, it's time to actually format that text. Let's start with font.

Fonts

Choosing a Font – General Thoughts

Word 2019 uses Calibri font as the default, but there are hundreds of fonts you can choose from and the font you use will govern the general appearance of the text in your document. Here is a sample of a few of those choices written in each font:

Sans-Serif Font Examples:

Calibri

Arial

Gill Sans MT

Serif Font Examples:

Times New Roman

Garamond

Palatino Linotype

The first three samples are sans-serif fonts. (That just means they don't have little feet at the bottom of the letters.) The second three samples are serif fonts. (They do have those little feet at the bottom of each letter.)

All of these fonts are the same size, but you can see that the different fonts have a different appearance and take up different amounts of space on the page. Arial is darker and taller than Calibri, for example.

Many corporations have a standard font they want you to use to be consistent with their brand and places like literary magazines will often specify which font to use for submitting stories. If that doesn't happen I'd suggest using a serifed font like Garamond or Times New Roman for main body text since a serifed font is supposed to be easier to read. Sans-serif fonts are good for headers or titles or for display text.

Also, unless you're working on a creative project, I'd recommend that you don't get too fancy with your fonts. Certain fonts, like Comic Sans, are so well-known for misuse that they are an immediate indicator that someone doesn't know design or isn't "professional."

The six fonts listed above are ones I'd generally consider safe.

Remember, at the end of the day, the goal is to communicate effectively, which means that a font like Algerian as main body text is not a good idea because readers will focus on the font and not the words.

Font Selection

Okay. So how do you change the font used in your document?

There are a few options.

But before we discuss those, let me point out that if you already know you want to use a different font, it's easier to change the font before you start typing. Once you do so, any new text will be in the new font.

Otherwise you'll need to select all of the text you want to change and then choose your font, which can be tricky if you're using different fonts for your headers and main body text

(A situation like that's also a good time to use Styles which is an intermediate-level topic covered in *Word 2019 Intermediate*.)

The first way to change the font is through the Font section of the Home tab. Click on the arrow to the right of the current font and choose a new one from the dropdown menu.

The first section of the dropdown menu lists the fonts for the theme you're using. Usually that'll be the defaults for Word, in this case, Calibri and Calibri Light.

Next you'll see Recently Used Fonts. (Most of the time there will only be one or two fonts there, but I had used a number recently.)

Finally, below those sections will be an alphabetical listing of all available fonts. If you know the font you want, you can start typing in its name rather than scroll through the entire list. Otherwise, use the scroll bar on the right-hand side or the up and down arrows to move through the list.

Each font is written using that font to give you an idea what it will look like. See for example the difference between Algerian and Garamond above.

The next way to change your font is to right-click and choose Font from the dropdown menu. This will bring up the Font dialogue box. In the top left corner you can choose the font you want.

There's a third option for changing the font, something I'm going to call the mini formatting menu. If you highlight your text it will appear on the screen when you let up on the left-click.

It will also appear above or below the dropdown menu if you right-click in your Word document.

As you can see, one of the options that you can change in the mini formatting menu is the font. In the example above, the current font is Arial, but I could click on the arrow on the right-hand side and change that. The dropdown menu looks the exact same as the one from the Font section of the Home tab we saw above.

Regardless of where you choose to change the font, if the font listing is blank that's because you have selected text that contains more than one font.

Font Size

Font size dictates how large the text will be. Here are some examples of different font sizes in Garamond font:

_{8 point} 12 point 16 point

As you can see, the larger the font size, the larger the text for that specific font. Most documents are written in a ten, eleven, or twelve point font size. Often footnotes or endnotes will use eight or nine point size. Chapter headings or title pages will use the larger font sizes.

Whatever font size you do use, try to be consistent between different sections of your document. So all main body text should use just one font size. Same for chapter or section headings.

Changing the font size works much the same way as changing the font. You have the same three options: You can go to the Font section of the Home tab, bring up the mini formatting menu by right-clicking or selecting your text, or bring up the Font dialogue box by right-clicking and choosing Font from the dropdown menu.

If you want to change existing text, you need to select the text first. Otherwise, change the font size before you start typing.

For all three options the current font size is listed to the right of the current font name in the Font section of the Home tab.

If you use the Home tab or the mini formatting menu there is a dropdown list of font sizes to choose from that you can see by clicking on the arrow next to the current font size. In the Font dialogue box that list of choices is already visible in a box under the current value.

If the font size you want isn't one of the choices listed you can type in the value you want instead by clicking into the box that shows the current font size and changing that number to the size you want just like you would with text in the main document.

With the Home tab and the mini formatting menu you can also increase your font size one listed value at a time by using the increase and decrease font options directly to the right of the font size.

These are depicted as the letter A with a small arrow above it that points either upward or downward. The one on the left with the arrow that points upward will increase the font size. The one on the right with the arrow that points downward will decrease the font size.

The values available with that option are the ones in the font size dropdown menu, so you can increase from 14 point to 16 point but not to 15 point using this option.

Font Color

Changing your font color works the same as changing your font or font size. Select the text you want to change and then either go to the Font section of the Home tab, pull up the mini formatting menu, or right-click and choose Font from the dropdown menu to bring up the Font dialogue box.

This time you want to click on the arrow next to the A with the solid colored line under it in the bottom right corner of the Font section:

That line is red by default but will change as you use the tool and will stay the mostly recently selected color until you close the document.

Clicking on the dropdown arrow will give you a dropdown menu with seventy different colors to choose from. Simply click on the color you want and it will change your selected text to that color.

If those seventy choices are not enough, you can click on More Colors at the bottom of the dropdown box to bring up the Colors dialogue box where you can choose from even more colors on the Standard tab or specify a color in the Custom tab using RGB or HSL values.

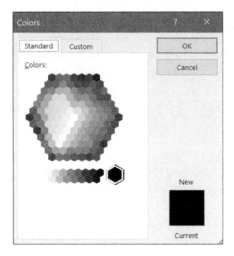

Once you select a font color any new text will be in that color. To go back to the default color choose Automatic from the dropdown menu.

Other Text Formatting

Highlight Text

You can also highlight text much like you might do with a highlighter using the Text Highlighter option which is located to the left of the Font Color option in the Font section of the Home tab or in the mini formatting menu. It has the letters ab and a pen with a colored line underneath.

By default the line is bright yellow but that changes as the tool is used.

To apply highlighting, select the text you want to highlight, and then either click on that option to highlight the text in the currently-displayed color or click on the dropdown arrow and choose from one of the fifteen color choices shown there.

To remove a highlight select the highlighted text, go to the highlight dropdown, and choose the No Color option. Once used, a highlight wil*l not* be applied to new text.

Bold Text

This is one you will probably use often. At least I do. As you can see with the headers in this chapter.

The easiest way to bold text is to use Ctrl + B.

You can use it before you start typing the text you want to bold or on a selection of text that you've chosen.

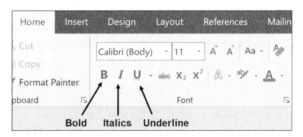

If you don't want to use the control keys, you can also go to the Font Section of the Home tab and click on the B on the left-hand side.

The final option is to select your text, right-click, choose Font from the dropdown menu, and then choose Bold in the Font Style section of the Font dialogue box.

(If you want to both bold and italicize text, you would choose Bold Italic.)

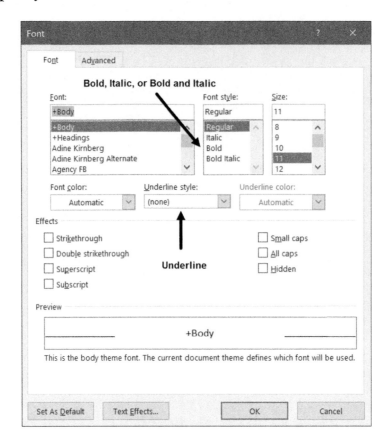

Italicize Text

To place text into italics—that means to have it sloped to the side like the subsection headers in this section for Italicize Text and Underline Text—the easiest way is to use Ctrl + I.

It works the exact same way as bolding text. You can do it before you type the letters or select the text and then use it.

Another option is to click on the slanted capital I in the Font section of the Home tab.

Or if you use the Font dialogue box select Italic under Font Styles. Or Bold Italic to have both italicized and bolded text.

Underline Text

Underlining text works much the same way as bolding or italicizing text.

The simplest way is to use Ctrl + U.

Or in the Font section of the Home tab you can click on the underlined U in the bottom row of the Font section.

There is also an Underline Style dropdown in the Font dialogue box.

Underline is different from italics and bold, however, because there are multiple underline options to choose from.

Using Ctrl + U will provide a single line underline of your text. So will just clicking on the U in the Font section of the Home tab. But if you click on the arrow next to the U in the Font section, you will see seven additional underline options to choose from including dotted and wavy lines.

Choosing More Underlines at the bottom of that list of options will open the Font dialogue box where you have a total of sixteen underline styles to choose from.

Remove Bolding, Underlining, or Italics

If you have bolded, underlined, or italicized text and you want to remove that formatting, you can simply select the text and use the command in question to remove that formatting.

So Ctrl + B, I, or U. Or you can click on the letter in the Font section of the Home tab or go to the Font dialogue box and remove the formatting from there.

If you select text that is partially formatted one way and partially formatted another—so say half of it is bolded and half is not—you will need to use the command twice. The first time will apply the formatting to all of the selected text, the second time will remove it from all of the selected text.

Also, with specialty underlining using Ctrl + U will initially revert the type of underlining to the basic single underline. To remove the underline altogether, you'll need to use Ctrl + U a second time.

Copy Formatting

Now for a text formatting trick that has saved me more times than I can count, the Format Painter.

Often in my corporate life I would find myself working on a group document where different sections were formatted differently. Usually it was a subtle difference such as the space between lines in a paragraph. Rather than guess and poke around trying to figure out what was causing the difference, I would use the Format Painter to copy the formatting from a "good" section to the rest of the document.

The Format Painter is located in the Clipboard section of the Home tab.

You can also access it in the mini formatting menu.

What it does is it takes all of the formatting from your selected text and applies it to the text you choose. This means color, font, font size, paragraph spacing, etc. All of it changes.

To use it, select the text with the formatting you want to copy (generally I select a whole paragraph or more), then click on Format Painter, then select the text you want to transfer the formatting to.

You need to use the mouse or trackpad to select the text you want to transfer your formatting to because using the arrow keys or the arrow and shift keys won't work

You'll know that the format painter is ready to transfer the format when you see a little paintbrush next to your cursor as you hover over your document. Format Painter in the Home tab will also be highlighted gray.

To turn it off without using it, use Esc.

If you double-click on the Format Painter it will remain available for use on multiple selections until you hit Esc or start typing in your document or click on it again.

A few more tips:

The format painter can be unreliable if there are different formats in the sample you're taking the formatting from. For example, if part of the text is red and part of the text is bolded and I format sweep from that sample to new text, only the formatting of the first letter in the sample will transfer.

Another issue worth mentioning. Sometimes with paragraph or numbered list formatting, I have to select the paragraph from the bottom instead of from the top in order to get the format painter to carry over the paragraph formatting I want. (This is also why I sometimes select multiple paragraphs.)

It's also possible to sweep formatting that's in one document to another document.

Last but not least, when you copy formatting over, *all* of the formatting in your target text will be removed. This can be an issue if you've used italics or bolding within a paragraph, for example.

That means you may have to go back and put the bold and italic formatting in manually, but sometimes Format Painter is the only way to get paragraphs formatted the same even when they appear to have the exact same settings in place.

Okay, then. On now to a discussion of paragraph formatting.

Paragraph Formatting

What we just discussed was basic text formatting. Now it's time to cover paragraph formatting which includes text alignment, line spacing, the space between paragraphs, indents, etc.

Here we're just going to discuss how to change the formatting of a specific paragraph but once you're comfortable enough in Word, I'd advise that you also learn to use Styles which will let you format one paragraph the way you want it, create a style from that paragraph, and then apply that Style to all other paragraphs that you want to have the same formatting. (It's covered in *Word 2019 Intermediate* or you can learn about it through Word's help function.)

Alright then. Let's talk about how to format a paragraph one element at a time.

Paragraphs

Alignment

There are four choices for paragraph alignment. Left, Center, Right, and Justified. The easiest way to choose your paragraph formatting option is via the Paragraph section of the Home tab. All four options are shown in the bottom row and are formatted to show the alignment they represent.

In the image below I've taken the same three-line paragraph and applied each alignment style to it to show the difference between all four using real paragraphs of text:

> This paragraph is **left-aligned**. And now I need to write enough additional text so that you can see what happens when a paragraph falls across multiple lines of text since that can be one of the most significant differences between the choices.
>
> This paragraph is **center-aligned**. And now I need to write enough additional text so that you can see what happens when a paragraph falls across multiple lines of text since that can be one of the most significant differences between the choices.
>
> This paragraph is **right-aligned**. And now I need to write enough additional text so that you can see what happens when a paragraph falls across multiple lines of text since that can be one of the most significant differences between the choices.
>
> This paragraph is **justified**. And now I need to write enough additional text so that you can see what happens when a paragraph falls across multiple lines of text since that can be one of the most significant differences between the choices.

Left-aligned, the first example, is how you'll often see text in documents. The text of each line is lined up along the left-hand side of the page and allowed to end in a jagged line on the right-hand side of the page.

Justified, the last example, is the other common way for text to be presented. Text is still aligned along the left-hand side, but instead of leaving the right-hand side ragged, Word adjusts the spacing between words so that all lines are also aligned along the right-hand side. (That's how the paragraphs in the print version of this book are formatted.)

Centered, the second example, is rarely used for full paragraphs of text like above, but is often used for section headers or titles or quotes. When text is centered the ends of each line are equally distant from the center of the line. You can end up with jagged left and right margins as a result and a final line, like above, may be substantially away from the edges.

Right-aligned, the third example above, is rare for paragraphs, at least in the U.S. and other countries where text goes from left to right. It aligns each line of text along the right-hand side and leaves the left-hand side ragged.

I have seen right-alignment used for text in side margins of non-fiction books and would expect to see it used for languages that read right to left.

So that's the difference between the choices. Like I said, I use Styles or the Home tab to change my paragraph alignment, but there are also control shortcuts that you can use. Ctrl + L will left-align, Ctrl + E will center your text,

Ctrl + R will right-align, and Ctrl + J will justify it. The only one I use enough to have memorized is Ctrl + E.

The third way to change your paragraph alignment is to select your text, right-click, and choose Paragraph from the dropdown menu to bring up the Paragraph dialogue box. The first option within that box is a dropdown where you can choose the alignment type you want. It has the exact same four formatting types that are available in the Home tab.

Spacing of a Single Paragraph

If you've ever attended school in the United States, you've probably been told at some point to submit a five-page paper that's double-spaced with one inch margins. Or if you've ever submitted a short story you were told to use a specific line spacing. In Word this is referred to as Line Spacing. So how do you do it?

As with the other formatting options, you can either do this before you start typing or by selecting the paragraphs you want to change after they've been entered into the document.

Once you're ready, go to the Paragraph section of the Home tab and locate the Line and Paragraph Spacing option. It's to the right of the paragraph alignment options and looks like five lines of text with two big blue up and down arrows on the left-hand side.

Click on the small black arrow to the right of the image to bring up the dropdown menu.

You have a choice of single-spaced (1.0) double-spaced (2.0), or triple-spaced (3.0) as well as 1.15, 1.5, and 2.5 spacing.

Below are examples of single, double, and triple-spaced paragraphs, Note how the amount of space between each row of text increases as you move from single-spaced up to triple-spaced:

This is a sample paragraph to show you the difference between line spacing. This is a **single-spaced** (1.0) paragraph. I'm going to keep typing so there are three lines of text to help you see the difference.

This is a sample paragraph to show you the difference between line spacing. This

is a **double-spaced** (2.0) paragraph. I'm going to keep typing so there are three

lines of text to help you see the difference.

This is a sample paragraph to show you the difference between line spacing. This

is a **triple-spaced** (1.0) paragraph. I'm going to keep typing so there are three lines

of text to help you see the difference.

If you want a different spacing than one of the dropdown options, then click on Line Spacing Options at the bottom of the list to bring up the Paragraph dialogue box.

You can go straight to the Paragraph dialogue box (shown in the next section) by right-clicking and choosing Paragraph from the dropdown menu. This setting is shown under the heading Line Spacing in the third section of the dialogue box which is labeled Spacing. It is on the right-hand side.

The dropdown menu gives you the choice of Single, 1.5, and Double as well as At Least, Exactly, and Multiple. Multiple lets you enter any value (such as 3 for triple-spacing). At Least and Exactly base the line spacing off of the number of points. So if you have 12 pt text, you can make the line spacing Exactly 12 point as well.

(This is often where I find that in corporate settings someone has tweaked the line spacing on a paragraph so that it doesn't match the rest of the paragraphs in the document. I usually fix it with the Format Painter, but if you don't want to use that, this is another setting to check.)

Okay. On to the spacing between paragraphs.

Spacing Between Paragraphs

There are basically two accepted ways to format paragraphs for most writing. One is what you see in the print version of this book where there are paragraphs without spacing between them but each new paragraph in a section after the first is indented to show that a new paragraph has begun. (Sometimes the first paragraph will also be indented.)

The second option is to start every paragraph on the left-hand side, but to add space between the lines to separate the paragraphs.

By default Word will add spacing between your paragraphs, but you can change the settings so that that does not happen or you can adjust the amount of space that Word adds.

Also, for items like titles or section headers (like you see on this page), it is better to add spacing to separate your text rather than use an extra blank line, because as your document adjusts to new text that extra line here or there can impact the appearance of the document. You may suddenly end up with a blank line on the top of the page that you never wanted there, for example.

And, please, for the love of everything, do not add lines between paragraphs by using enter unless the document is just for you or will only be seen by someone else in a printed format. That's about as bad as using the tab key to indent your paragraphs. (Don't do that either. Use indenting which we'll talk about next.)

Okay, so where do you go to adjust the spacing between your paragraphs? If all you want to do is remove any existing spacing, you can do that in the same dropdown we looked at above. It's the Remove Space After Paragraph option.

If someone has already removed the space after a paragraph and all you want to do is add it back in, you can also use that dropdown and select Add Space After Paragraph. (It's not listed above because there was already a space for the paragraph I was working with, but if your paragraph does not have a space after it, that will be an option you can choose.)

Be careful with the dropdown because it also, as you can see above, can have an Add Space Before Paragraph option. That will put the space above your paragraph as opposed to below it.

M.L. Humphrey

For this one, though, I tend to work in the Paragraph dialogue box which you can access by choosing Line Spacing Options in the dropdown or by right-clicking and choosing Paragraph from the dropdown menu in the main workspace:

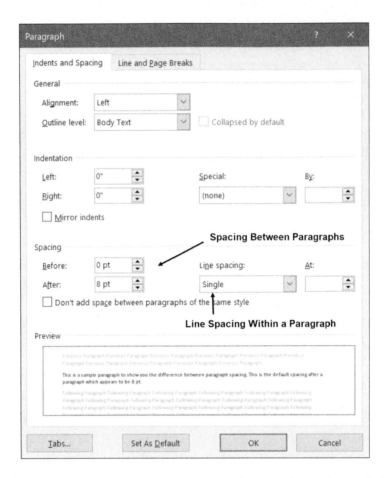

The spacing between paragraphs options are in the third section of the dialogue box, which is labeled Spacing, and on the left-hand side. There is a box for Before and one for After.

If you set your paragraphs to have spacing both before and after, the space between two paragraphs will be the higher of those two values not the combination of them. (So if you say 12 point before and 6 point after, the spacing between them will be 12 point not 18 point.)

If you just wanted spacing at the top of a section of paragraphs or at the bottom of a section of paragraphs but not between them, you can click the box to say don't add spacing to paragraphs of the same style Another option is to just add paragraph spacing to that top-most or bottom-most paragraph (although if you're working with Styles I wouldn't recommend that because you can accidentally override it.)

Below are examples of different paragraph spacing after paragraphs. I have no spacing, the default space that you get from the dropdown which is 8 pt, and 14 pt spacing just to show a visual difference. Because this is a screenshot they may not in fact be 8 and 14 pt spaces, but you can see the relative difference in appearance between each one.

> This is a sample paragraph to show you the difference between paragraph spacing. There is **no spacing** after this paragraph.
> This is a sample paragraph to show you the difference between paragraph spacing. This is the **default spacing** after a paragraph which appears to be 8 pt.
>
> This is another sample paragraph to show you the difference between paragraph spacing. This time I'm going to put a **14 pt space** after this paragraph.
>
> And this is final paragraph so you can see the spacing above.

Usually if I set a spacing I don't go above the font point size. The above font was 11 point in the document I was using, so in that case my spacing would normally be no more than 11 pt. (If I was writing a large-print document that might not be the case, so know your audience and the standards for that audience.)

Okay. So that was spacing within paragraphs and then spacing between paragraphs. As I mentioned above, if you have no spacing between paragraphs, the standard for indicating a new paragraphs is to add an indent to the first line of each new paragraph. Let's discuss how to do that now.

Indenting

Word provides two indenting options in the Paragraph section of the Home tab, but neither one will not give the first-line indent we need. They move the entire paragraph in or out.

For indenting a single line you need to use the Paragraph dialogue box which can be opened by right-clicking within your document and choosing Paragraph from the dropdown menu.

The second section of the dialogue box is labeled Indentation and covers whole paragraph and single line indents.

The whole paragraph indent options are on the left-hand side. The single-line or hanging indent option (which indents all but the first line of a paragraph) options are on the right-hand side.

Here I have settings for a paragraph with a first line indent:

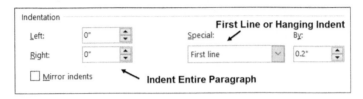

And here are examples of the various indenting choices:

> This is a paragraph with **no indentation**. I am now going to make it long enough so that you can see what happens with the second line as well.
>
> This is a paragraph with a **left indent of .2"**. I am now going to make it long enough so that you can see what happens with the second line.
>
> This is a paragraph with a **right indent of .2"**. I am now going to make it long enough so that you can see what happens with the second line.
>
> This is a paragraph where the **first line has an indent of .2"** but the rest of the paragraph has no indent added.
>
> This is a paragraph where the indent is a **hanging indent of .2"** but the rest of the paragraph has no indent added.

The first example above has no paragraph indent.

The second and third show indents from the left and right-hand sides, respectively. Each is indented by .2" and you can see that on the side where it's indented it either starts or ends earlier than the non-indented paragraph.

(I formatted the paragraphs as Justified so that they'd fit the entire line and make that difference more obvious.)

The fourth example has the first line indented, but the remaining lines would not be. So you can see that "added" on the second line is as far left as the unindented paragraph at the top.

The final example is of a hanging indent where the first line is not indented, but the second and any subsequent lines would be.

To indent an entire paragraph, change the value for Left or Right on the left-hand side of the Indentation section.

To indent just the first line of a paragraph, choose First Line from the dropdown menu under Special on the right-hand side of the Indentation section and then specify by how much in the By box.

To create a hanging indent, choose Hanging from the Special dropdown and then specify the amount in the By box.

Remember to either do this in advance or to select the existing paragraphs you want to change before you start making your changes.

As I mentioned above, there are increase and decrease indent options in the Paragraph section of the Home tab. They're on the top row and show a series of lines with blue arrows pointing either to the left (to decrease an indent) or the right (to increase an indent).

They allow you to increase or decrease the indent for a paragraph or an entire selection of text from the left-hand side.

In my version of Word it indents by .5" the first time, then to a 1" indent the second time, and then to a 1.5" indent the third time.

If there are other indented paragraphs in the document, such as the ones I added before that had a .2" indent, then it will indent to those points as well.

When you decrease the indent it should follow the same stopping points on the way back to zero.

I will often use these quick indent options when dealing with a bulleted or numbered list that I want to visually separate from the main text of my document.

Lists

Bulleted

A bulleted list is just what it sounds like, a list of items where each line starts with some sort of marker or bullet on the left-hand side. The most common bullet choice is probably a small dark black circle that's filled in, but Word has additional options you can choose from such as an open circle, a filled-in square, and a checkmark. (See image below.)

You can either start a bulleted list before you have your items ready or you can take a list of items, highlight them, and then apply a bulleted list.

With either option, the way to do this is to go to the Paragraph section of the Home tab and click on the arrow next to the bulleted list option to bring up a dropdown menu where you can select the type of bullet you want.

If you simply click on the image of the bulleted list instead of using the dropdown menu, your bullet will be a solid black circle.

Here are samples of each of the bullet choices shown above. (I had to create this by going into each line and choosing a different bullet type for that line. The default with bulleted lists is that once you choose a bullet that will be the bullet used for every line.)

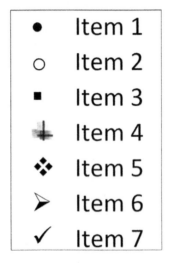

When you choose to insert a bulleted list, if you don't have any text selected already then a single bullet will appear on the page where your cursor was, waiting for you to type in your first entry.

If you do have items selected, each paragraph will be indented and the bullet type you chose will be added at the beginning of each of the paragraphs.

The mini formatting menu also has the bulleted list option available in the middle of the bottom row, so that's another option for applying or removing a bulleted list.

Once you've started a bulleted list each time you hit enter at the end of the text for a bulleted entry a new bullet will appear on the next line for you to add your next item.

Hit enter twice to return to normal paragraph indenting with no bullet. If you add a new bulleted list and then don't type any text before you hit enter again that will also revert back to no bullet.

(The double enter trick works for the first level of bullets. If you have a list with multiple levels of bullets, which we're about to cover, then you will need to hit enter until Word works its way through the levels of bullets and back to a blank option.)

You can create a bulleted list with multiple levels by using the Tab key to indent any line you want to the next level. Like so:

Here I've created three levels of indented text. I started with my first bullet and typed my text, then hit enter after Level 1. Next I used the tab to move that solid bullet in one level and create a second-level bullet. I then typed my text for that level and hit enter. And then repeated the process of tab, type, enter to create the other levels.

By default, when you hit enter from an existing line of a bulleted list the next line will be indented at that same level and will use the bullet mark for that level of indent.

To decrease an indent one level you can use Shift- + Tab.

When using Tab or Shift + Tab, if that line already has text in it be sure to place your cursor before any text. In the examples above, that would mean place it to the left of the first L in Level.

When you create a multi-level bulleted list, Word assigns a different bullet type for each indented level.

From what I can tell it uses the open circle for the first indented bullet, the black square for the second one, and then the black circle for the third one regardless of which option you chose for your first bullet. (See above.)

It then starts over again with the open circle for the next-level indent.

To change the bullet style for any level in your list, click on that line and go to the bulleted list options and choose a new bullet type.

That will apply that new bullet type to all lines in your list that are indented at that level. So, for example, all second-level indents will have the same bullet type and if you change that type for one line it will change it for *all* second-level indents in your list even if they are not listed together.

To remove bullets from a list, select the list, and then click on the bulleted list option in the Home tab or mini formatting menu. Your bullets will be removed, but the text will remain indented.

Another option for removing a bullet is to go to the beginning of the text for that line and backspace. Once will remove the bullet but keep the text where it is. Twice will move the text to the beginning of the line.

(You can also use the Format Painter to apply bullets to a list of entries or to remove them.)

With bulleted lists, Word will automatically indent your bullet and text when it adds the bullet for the first level. If you don't want that, you can use the Decrease Indent option to move the bullet back to the left-hand side of the page but keep the bullets.

If you decrease the indent for the first level of a multi-level bulleted list, this moves all levels back one indent.

The same works for increasing the indent using the Home tab option. If you increase the indent for the first level, it will increase the indent for all levels.

(For levels below that first level using Decrease Indent or Increase Indent just moves that specific line forward or backward one indent.)

You can also use the Paragraph dialogue box to have more control over how much each line is indented and whether each bulleted line should be treated as a hanging paragraph or not.

Another option you can use for indenting is the Adjust List Indents option from the dropdown menu on the main workspace. That will bring up the Adjust List Indents dialogue box.

This dialogue box allows you to choose the indent amount for the bullet. (It also is available for numbered lists, which we'll talk about next.)

The first choice is how much to indent the bullet or number.

The second choice is how much to indent the associated text.

The third choice is what type of separator to use between the bullet or number and the text. The default is a tab but you can also choose to use a space or nothing.

The choices you make here are probably more finicky for numbered lists than they are for bulleted lists since the bullet size remains constant no matter how many entries you have in your list. With numbered lists you have to move from 1 through 9 to 10 to 99 and then to 100 on which requires different amounts of space so each change can create a difference in the appearance of the list.

One more thing to note and then we'll move on to numbered lists.

I often will use the Paragraph dialogue box to add extra line spacing between bulleted list entries since sometimes I think entries in a list look better with a little more spacing between them than is used in a normal paragraph.

Numbered

A numbered list is similar to a bulleted list except the entries are either labeled with numbers or letters. If you've ever had to provide an outline of a paper for school, I'm sure you've run across a numbered list before.

One easy way to create a numbered list is to simply type the first number you want to use, the separator mark you want, and then a space.

So, for example, if I type a capital A and then a period and then a space that will give me the first entry in a numbered list that uses A, B, C, D, etc.

When I do that, Word automatically indents that text and turns it into the first entry in a numbered list so that when I type in my text and then hit enter the next line will be "numbered" in sequence and indented as well.

(If Word ever does that to you and you don't want it to indent and start creating a list, just use Ctrl + X to Undo. You can also click on the little AutoCorrect dropdown that appears to the left-hand side of the entry and choose to undo from there.)

The other option, especially if you already have your text entered and just need to convert it to a numbered list, is to select the lines you want to number, go to the Paragraph section of the Home tab, click on the arrow next to the Numbering option, and choose the numbered list option you want from there.

As you can see, you have the option to choose between lists that use

1, 2, 3

i, ii, iii

I, II, III

A, B, C

a, b, c

and then between using a period (.) or a paren( )) as the separator.

For a basic list, that should be all you really need. The default numbering choice if you just click on the image instead of using the dropdown is 1, 2, 3 separated with a period.

(In addition to the Home tab, the mini formatting menu also has the numbered list option.)

As with bulleted lists, you can create a multi-level list by using the tab key to indent a line or paragraph in your numbered list, but there appears to be that same pre-defined order for what will be used for each of the indented levels.

For the first indent Word uses the lower-case letters (a, b, c). For the second indent it uses lower-case Roman numerals (i, ii, iii). For the third indent it uses regular numbers (1, 2, 3). And then it cycles through again starting with the fourth-level indent. Like so:

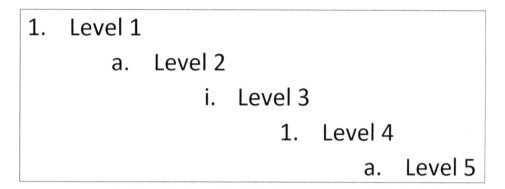

1. Level 1
    a. Level 2
        i. Level 3
            1. Level 4
                a. Level 5

This generally results in a multi-level list that doesn't fit what I was taught in school which was I, A, 1, a, i for the numbering order for different levels.

To create a list with customized numbering in each level, you'd need to use the Multilevel List option which we are not covering here because it has given me more problems over the years than probably anything else I've ever worked with in Word.

(It's the option to the right of the number list option in the Paragraph section if you want to experiment with it and I do reluctantly cover it in *Word 2019 Intermediate*.)

For now, back to basic numbered lists.

If you had a numbered list earlier in your document and want that numbering to continue with additional numbered items later in your document, you can do that. Likewise if Word continued the numbering and you didn't want it to, you can change the settings to restart the numbering.

In either case, create your numbered list and then right-click on the number for the line you want to change.

Depending on what else is in your document and which entry you click on, you will see different options in the dropdown menu.

Restart at 1 or Restart at A will change the number of the entry to 1 or A or whatever the first value would be for that numbering type. All you have to do is click on this one for it to be applied.

Continue Numbering is also applied immediately. Click on it to continue the numbering from the last time that numbering type was used. So if you have a list in your document that has the "numbers" A, B, C and another list that has numbering of 1 and 2 and the numbering style on your current line is the A, B, C style then when you choose to continue numbering your next entry will be D even if the 1 and 2 values are closer to that line in the document.

(If it sounds confusing, just play around with it in Word and you'll see what I'm talking about.)

The final option you'll see is Set Numbering Value which will bring up the Set Numbering Value dialogue box when you choose it.

This gives you the most control over what happens with your list numbering. You can restart the list, continue numbering, continue numbering with skipped numbers, or start numbering at any value you want.

If you do set the numbering at a random value, just be aware that your choices are based upon the list type for that line. So if it's a level that's numbered with Roman numerals then you'd have to use X for 10, you couldn't type in 10.

Be a little careful with all of this because a change to the numbering style of one entry will change all other linked lines which is great when that's what you want but can be dangerous if you're working with a very large document and don't realize that the list on page fifty is somehow tied into the list on page ten.

Always if you're working with numbered lists be sure to go back through your entire document at the end to make sure that a change you made towards the end of the document didn't change something at the beginning of the document.

(This actually goes for page or section breaks as well. Best practice is to always do one last read through or scan of a document after all changes have been made and to restart that scan from the beginning if you end up making more changes.)

Okay. A few final points. As with bulleted lists you can change the indent and format of your numbered list using the Paragraph dialogue box or the Adjust List Indents option on the dropdown menu.

Also, I mentioned it above, but one thing to be careful of with numbered lists that go into the double-digits or triple-digits is that you can end up with a situation where the text is lined up for values of 1 through 9 but then not aligned once you reach a value of 10 or more.

This can happen, for example, when you use a space instead of a tab to follow the number, but I want to say that I've also seen it happen with tabs if the tabs were set in such a way that it changed which tab stop was used for 1 through 9 versus 10.

Also, it won't be an issue most times, but if you hold your mouse over the numbered list options that Word gives you by default some are right-aligned and some are left-aligned. As you move into larger and large values for your numbered list this may impact the appearance of your list.

To fix this, you'll need to create a New Number Format where you can customize the alignment. That option is at the bottom of the dropdown menu under Define New Number Format. (See screenshot on next page.)

Click on that and it will bring up the Define New Number Format dialogue box where you can choose the number style, number format (whether to use a period or paren or something else even), and the number alignment.

So, for example, the default for 1,2,3 is left-aligned. But you could use this option to make it right-aligned or centered. Here are what those three options look like for numbered values of 9 and 10:

9.   Level 1 Left-Aligned
10. Level 2 Left-Aligned
9.   Level 1 Centered
10. Level 2 Centered
9.   Level 1 Right-Aligned
10. Level 2 Right-Aligned

The only change I made here is in the alignment of the numbers. You can see in the first example that the 9 lines up with the 1 in 10. In the second sample it lines up with the center of the 10. And in the third example it lines up with the 0 in the 10. Personally I prefer the right-aligned version. But the default is left-aligned, so the only way to get this is to create your own number format using Define New Number Format.

One nice thing in Word is that once you've used a number format in a document that format is available for you to select again in the Document Number Formats section in the Numbering dropdown menu of the Home tab or the mini formatting menu.

Although one weird thing about that section is that it will show formats you've used at one point but are no longer using. For example, in this screenshot I only have numbered lists in my document right now but it's showing lists with a, b, c, and A, B, C, and I, II, III even though they're not currently in use anywhere in the document.

(One of the reasons I'm careful with playing around with lists in a working document.)

In the case above where I had three different number formats for the 1, 2, 3 numbering you can't tell which is which just from looking. You have to hold your mouse over each one to figure out which one has each alignment.

You could also click on a line that already has that format and see which one of the formats in the dropdown is then surrounded by a dark gray border.

Or you could just use the Format Painter to copy the number formatting over, which is probably what I would actually do instead.

Other Tips & Tricks

Alright. We've talked about how to enter text into Word and how to format that text once you've entered it and how to format your paragraphs. But there are a few more basics we need to cover that don't really have anything to do with entering or formatting your text, although they may lead to changes in your text.

Let's start with Find and Replace.

Find and Replace

Find

If you ever want to find a particular word or phrase in a Word document and you don't want to scan through the whole document, you'll need to use Find. It's very easy to use on the surface, but can also be incredibly powerful if you get into the specialty search options.

For a basic search in Word you can use Ctrl + F or just go to the Navigation task pane on the left-hand side of the workspace. If the Navigation pane is already open then using Ctrl + F will seem like it did nothing, but what it will actually do is place your cursor in the Search Document box in the Results section of the Navigation pane.

(In older versions of Word using Ctrl + F opened the Find and Replace dialogue box so this one throws me every single time.)

If all you're looking for is a simple word or phrase, type it into the search box. You don't even need to hit enter, all instances of the search term will be listed immediately right below the search box. Like so:

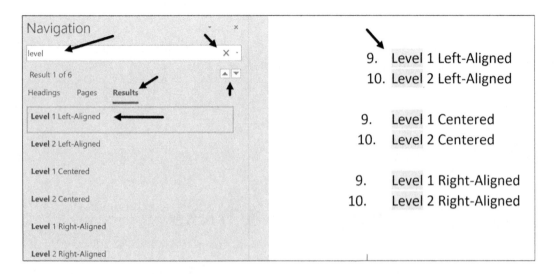

The gray area on the left-hand side is the Navigation pane where I entered "level" as my search term. Immediately below that are the six search results for the document. It bolds the location of the text and provides some of the text around that to make it easy to determine which search result you want.

On the right-hand side is the document itself. Each instance of the search term is highlighted in yellow.

For a larger document where all of the search results are not on the same page, you can simply click on the search result in the list that you want to see and Word will take you to that page. You can also use the up and down arrows just below the far end of the search box (in the same row as the number of search results) to move through your search results one-by-one.

Click on the X at the end of the search box to clear the search result.

Right next to that X is a small dropdown arrow with a list of additional search options. Click on the arrow and one of the first choices is "Advanced Find".

The dropdown is available even if you haven't searched for anything. In that case the X is replaced with a magnifying glass.

Clicking on that Advanced Find option will open the Find and Replace dialogue box which lets you search for far more than just a word or phrase.

I usually get to the same place by using Ctrl + H (which is the control shortcut for replace) and then clicking over to the Find portion of the dialogue box. Either way what you will then see is this:

Type your search phrase into the Find What search bar and then click on Find Next to walk your way through the entire document and look at each instance of your search term.

For a basic search the Navigation pane is the far better choice.

But click on that More button in the bottom left corner of the Find dialogue box and you get this:

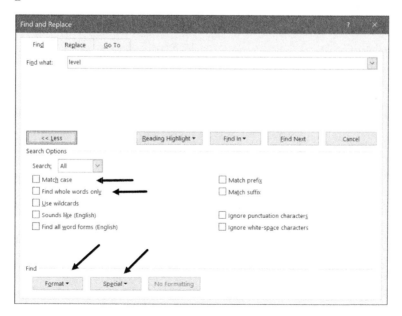

There are a ton of additional search options you can use, but I want to focus on four of them right now.

First, is Match Case. Which is in the Search options section in the middle.

Match Case will look at the search term you enter and only find words with the same capitalization. So if you search for "CAT" and you check this box it will only locate "CAT" for you not "cat" or "Category".

(For my old job something like that would be useful since CAT stood for consolidated audit trail.)

When searching for a proper name or an abbreviation like that, I recommend always checking this box. (This becomes even more important if you're going to use Replace. You wouldn't want to try to replace CAT with some other term and accidentally also replace the cat portion of category with that same term, for example.)

The next option I want to point out is Find Whole Words Only.

Find Whole Words Only will only search for the entire word you enter. So again, with the example of "CAT", if you just searched Word normally it would return any word that has "cat" in it. So "category" and "implication" would be returned along with "CAT" and "cat."

By using Find Whole Words Only the search results would be limited to "CAT" and "cat". You can also combine these two and then your only result would be the one for CAT.

So those are great. And I've saved myself a lot of time over the years by using them.

But a few that I only started using in recent years may be even more powerful than that when they're needed.

At the bottom of the dialogue box are Format and Special dropdown options. Here's what the Format one gives you for choices if you click on it:

A little hard to see maybe, but the options are Font, Paragraph, Tabs, Language, Frame, Style, and Highlight.

Using these options you can search your document for pretty much any format, paragraph style, text style, or highlight that you want. Here's what comes up when you choose Font for example:

Look at all those options.

Now, that may not sound exciting to you, but let me give you a weird example of where I've needed to use this:

For large-print books they don't use italics, they use bolded text instead. I recently published a seven-hundred-page book in large print. Manually going through that book to find each instance of italics would've been a nightmare. But I was able to easily use find (and replace) to change all of my italics over to bolded text in the space of a minute.

Another time I've needed this is when I've been working on a report and someone decided that all uses of a specific term needed to be in italics or not in italics.Using Format I could search for instances of the term that were not formatted properly. Far easier than looking at every single use of the term one-by-one.

If you know your control shortcuts, you can skip the dropdown and use them directly in the search box.

Just click into the search box and use, for example, Ctrl + I. The first time the search will change to search for that formatting. The second time it will change to search for text that does not have that formatting. The third time it will go back to a neutral search. Which state you're in will show directly below the search box.

To find all text in a document with a specific format, like italics, just leave the search box blank. Don't enter any text. But do use the Ctrl + I or whatever shortcut it is to specify that format. When you click on search Word will show you all of the the text with that specific format.

Also, be careful when using the formatting search options that you don't forget to change your search back to neutral because next time you search you may end up missing a search result. It doesn't happen often, but it has happened to me in the past at least in older versions of Word.

The final one I wanted to point out is right next to the Format option and that is the Special option.

The Special search dropdown allows you to search for specific formatting marks in your document such as paragraph marks, em dashes, en dashes, etc.

This can be a lifesaver if someone gives you a document where they used Enter multiple times instead of using a page break or used tabs to indent paragraphs instead of formatting the paragraph properly.

Maybe most people won't run into needing these options, but if you've ever been the one stuck with a group report that has to be fixed to make everything work properly chances are there's something in this section that will make your life easier.

Replace

Okay. So that's Find which is helpful, but where the real power of Find comes into play is when you pair it with Replace. So not only do you find that italicized text, but you replace it with bolded text at the same time.

Same with fixing two spaces after a period. I was raised to type two spaces after a period but there are members of the younger generation (and even some of my own) who think that using two spaces after a period makes you an archaic fool stuck in the typewriter age. Rather than engage in heated debate about something that really no one should care about, I just used Find and Replace to find all instances of two spaces after a period and replace them with one space.

Easy.

(And I will add that I finally converted from two spaces to one space when I started publishing printed books because when you use justified paragraphs like I am in the print version of this book that extra space after a sentence can created some ugly white space on the page. But honestly, even though I've converted I think it's one of those silly issues people use to distinguish those who are "in the know" from those who are not and I hate that kind of thing with a burning passion. But I digress.)

Back to find and replace. It is fantastic and powerful and will save you so much time. But it's easy to mess up and create horrible and strangely embarrassing errors.

So before you replace every instance of something in your document in one step, make sure that you've thought through what that means.

Let's say I want to replace CAT with SEC CAT. I know I'm not using "cat" in the report I've written, but what about implication, category, catastrophe, etc. If I don't realize that replacing "cat" with "SEC CAT" can affect those words, too, I might be tempted to not constrain my replacements to match the case and to whole words only. In which case I will have SEC CATastrophe in my document somewhere and impliSEC CATion.

Not what you want, so always think it through first.

Okay. So the basics of find and replace:

Use either use Ctrl + H or go to the Editing section of the Home tab and click on Replace to bring up the Find and Replace dialogue box, which will open onto the Replace tab.

The Find What box is the exact same as before and you can click on the More option in the bottom right corner to specify Match Case, Whole Words Only, any formatting, etc. for what you want to find.

There will now be a Replace With box below that where you type what you want to replace that text with. So if CAT needs to become SEC CAT I would type CAT in the Find What box and SEC CAT in the Replace With box. (And be sure to check the whole word and match case boxes as well.)

Another example: If I were replacing two spaces with one I'd type two spaces in the Find What box and one space in the Replace With box.

You then have two choices for how to replace text. You can replace the instances of your search term one one at time by using Find Next and then clicking on Replace once you confirm that you want to use replace. Or you can use Replace All to replace all instances of your search term with your Replace With term at once.

(I recommend double-checking you got it right if you do use Replace All.)

As mentioned above, you can find one type of formatting and replace it with another type of formatting. So I can find italics and replace it with bold, for example. To do this, click into the search and replace boxes and use the relevant control shortcuts for the formatting you want to find and the formatting you want to replace it with.

One other item to note. When Word finds and replaces, it will sometimes do so only from where you are in the document forward. When this happens it tells you how many items it found and replaced and then asks if you want to continue searching from the beginning. To be sure that you've found all instances, say yes.

This means you can also do find and replace on just a highlighted section of text, too, which is sometime very useful. In that instance when it asks if you want it to continue with the rest of the document, say no.

Spelling and Grammar Check

Unless you've done something to your settings or are working in a document that's already hundreds of pages long, you'll notice little red squiggly lines or blue double-underlines appear under some words as you type.

This is Word's real-time spelling and grammar check at work.

> To be fair, she wasn't actually trying to pee on her toy, but in Fancyworld there wasn't a good cause and effect connection in place. So it always went: smell something interesting, drop toy to smell it better, step forward to pee on something interesting while forgetting that the toy that was just dropped is right there, too.
>
> I tell ya, that girl keeps me on my toes.

It may be a little hard to see, but in the screenshot above Word flagged Fancyworld and ya as spelling mistakes by placing a squiggly red line under each word and the use of So as a grammar error by placing a double blue line under it.

For spelling errors, right-click and Word will suggest possible spellings at the top of the dropdown menu.

Here, for example, Word suggested using yam, yak, yaw, a, and yet instead of ya. Which actually highlights a key point with using the spelling and grammar check. Word can't always tell what you were trying to do. So in this case "ya" is slang usage for "you" but that never even made the list of suggestions.

The dictionary that Word works from does not contain slang, but when writing fiction, for example, you may find yourself using lots of slang, especially in dialogue. So spellcheck is great and you should use it for every single document you ever give to anyone else, but it has its limits. Do not blindly follow the recommendations.

Not even the grammar recommendations. I have seen the grammar check suggest using its when it's was actually the correct usage. It is not infallible.

But it is helpful.

More so for business or school writing than fiction or casual writing, although you can at least customize your dictionary if you want. In the dropdown shown above you can see that there is an option to Add To Dictionary which if you choose it will add that word to your Word dictionary so that it is never flagged as a misspelling again. (In business settings I will often add my first name to the dictionary because Word flags it every time and wants to change it to something that would not be good in a business setting.)

In general, though, I don't add words to the dictionary. I would rather in each document use the Ignore All choice.

This is mostly because I can't think through every possible usage of a word to make sure there wouldn't be times when it was in fact a misspelling of some other word. For example, what if I had a document that used the word yam in it and I really did misspell it once as ya. I'd miss that if I had added ya to the dictionary.

Bottom line: Don't do something permanent unless you're sure of what you're doing.

A few more things to know about spellcheck:

Sometimes it flags a word as misspelled when it isn't. I've found that I have one or two words in each novel I write that it flags that are genuine words but aren't listed in the default dictionary. I verify the word is spelled and used correctly with a quick internet search before I ignore the error.

Also, if you're not close enough to the right spelling Word can't help you. I used to consistently spell bureaucracy in such a way that it had no idea what word I was trying to write.

For grammar errors, Word will also suggest an immediate fix. I usually leave those until the end when I can run the Spelling and Grammar check on the entire document at once.

And again, sometimes the suggestions it makes aren't the actual problem. For example, above with "so" its suggestion was to keep the so but put a comma after it which to me is simply a different pacing for that sentence that I don't like as much. What it should actually suggest is that I not use so so many times.

(See what I did there? Haha.)

Unless Word has flagged a blatant spelling error I tend not to worry about any of this until I'm done with the entire document and then I run through it all at once. Stopping every single time Word flags a potential issue would bring me out of my writing flow and make me far less efficient. (For those who cannot continue if they know there's an error in what they've already written those lines can be very useful, though.)

Of course, if your document is long enough you will eventually get a message that it had to stop real-time tracking of spelling and grammar errors. I want to say this happens somewhere around one hundred pages.

Okay, then. For those who want to wait until the end and do it all at once, you do not have to scroll through your document and try to find every one of these.

You can use the Spelling & Grammar option which is in the Proofing section of the Review tab on the left-hand side.

Once you click on that option, Word will open a Proofing pane on the right-hand side of your workspace and will show the next grammar or spelling error in the document. (It doesn't automatically start at the top. If you had a selection of text highlighted it will focus on that selected text. If you're clicked somewhere in the document it will work from there forward.)

Here is the result for the grammar error for "so" that we discussed before:

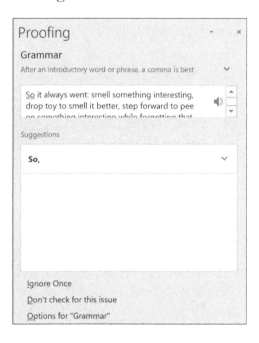

At the top it describes the issue, then it displays a snippet of text around the word or usage that was flagged, and then below that in the Suggestions section shows suggested fixes for the error.

Likewise, here is the Proofing pane for the "ya" spelling error.

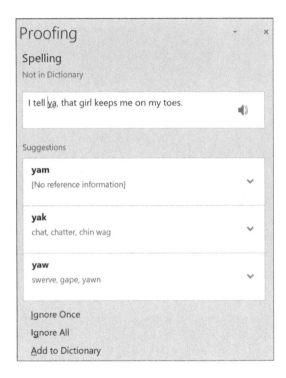

If you agree that there is an error, you can just click on the suggested fix you want and Word will make that edit to your document for you.

If you agree that there's an error but want to fix it some other way, you can click back into your document and make the edit yourself.

If you don't believe there's an error, then at the bottom of the screen you can click on Ignore Once and Word will move on to the next grammar or spelling error.

With spelling errors you can choose to Ignore All and it will not flag that word again in the document but spellcheck sometimes will still flag related uses of a word such as a possessive, singular, plural, or upper or lower case.

For example, it treated all of these as separate words that had to be ignored individually: Winswald Winswalds Winswald's winswald winswald's winswalds.

With grammar errors you can click on Don't Check for This Error. Just be sure that you really want that to happen. Just because it was wrong on this particular instance does not mean it will always be wrong and the listed grammar rules tend to be high-level.

You can see what the grammar error is by looking at the top of the pane. In the case above it says, "After an introductory word or phrase, a comma is best." Before choosing to skip that rule I'd have to believe that there are never any introductory phrases I use where a comma is warranted but I failed to include one. I'm not comfortable deciding that so I'd let it stand.

The final option for spelling in the Proofing page is to add the word to the dictionary, which we already discussed.

The final option for grammar is to see the grammar options. When you click on that choice Word will bring up the Grammar Settings dialogue box.

The first screen worth of options are pretty standard and they're all on by default. I don't think any of these give me enough problems that I'd need to turn one off, but you could. The capitalization one can be a little annoying when writing about Excel functions, but otherwise pretty standard stuff.

Where it gets interesting is if you scroll down to the categories for Clarity, Conciseness, Formality, Inclusiveness, Punctuation Conventions, and Vocabulary.

(Now, whether I really want developers who won't use Title Case for their text labels to be telling me about proper word usage is up for debate, but there are some interesting options in those sections.).

For example, in more formal settings, such as academic writing, contractions are frowned upon. The Formality section includes the ability to check your document for those.

So if you are writing an academic paper and want to be sure you didn't accidentally include a contraction, you can have Word check that for you.

There's even a setting for the Oxford comma as well as one for checking for the number of spaces between sentences.

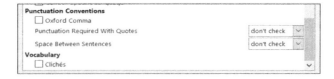

If any of that looks interesting to you, you can go into the Grammar Setup dialogue box and turn those options on by checking the relevant boxes.

Or if one of those rules keeps coming up and you don't want it to, this is the place to fix that.

One final note, once you've run spellcheck on a document and told Word to ignore spelling or grammar errors, it will continue to ignore those errors in that document. To run a clean spelling and grammar check of your document, go to the File tab, click on Options, click on Proofing, and finally click on the gray box labeled Recheck Document.

This will show you a notice that you're about to reset the spelling and grammar check. Click OK and all spelling and grammar errors will be flagged as they were originally.

Synonyms and Thesaurus

In the screenshot above where I showed you the Spelling & Grammar option you may have noticed that there was a Thesaurus option next to it.

A thesaurus, as you may know, is used to identify words with a similar or identical meaning, otherwise known as synonyms.

If I've used "happy" ten times and want to come up with a different word for it, I can use the thesaurus option in Word to find one.

The simplest way to do this is to right-click on the word and go to the synonyms choice in the dropdown menu and then look at the available options listed there:

If you like one of the choices simply click on it and your existing text will be replaced with the chosen word.

You can also select your word and then use the Thesaurus option from the Proofing section of the Review tab to open a Thesaurus task pane on the right-hand side of the workspace.

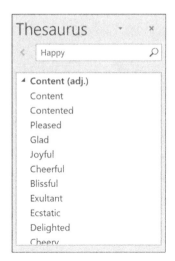

As you can see, at least in this instance, there are more choices provided in the Thesaurus task pane than there were in the synonyms dropdown menu.

The Thesaurus appears to work differently, however. If you click on one of the words listed it does not replace the word in your document but instead will provide synonyms for that word instead.

To insert the word into your document as a replacement you need to hold your mouse over the word so that it's highlighted, go to the end of the line where that word is, click on the dropdown arrow, and choose insert.

If you had a word or words highlighted in your document it or they will be replaced. If not, the new word will be inserted into the document where your cursor was.

Let me just step back for a moment and give a general caution about using a thesaurus. It's fantastic when what you're doing is triggering your memory of other similar words and you can go down the list and think about each one like a puzzle piece that you're trying to fit into place with what you're writing.

But it is a very bad idea to use a thesaurus to find words you don't already know.

For example, here with happy. One of the options is blissful. Another is exultant. But both of those convey a level of emotion that is not, in my mind, equivalent to being happy. And pleasant, which is another suggested word goes in the wrong direction. Someone is a pleasant person to be around but that is not the same thing as their being a happy person. One is what I feel around that person, another is what they feel.

(If that makes sense. I don't write dictionaries, so forgive me if my example there was bad.) The point is, you have to still know the words you choose when using a thesaurus or it's just not going to sound right.

But if you do need to use it, that's how.

Word Count

The other item in the Proofing section of the Review tab that I want to mention is Word Count. When I was in school we always had to hit a page limit, but for short stories and novels and online forms everyone wants to know the word count.

There are two main places you can find this. The first is actually just in the bottom left-hand corner of the Word screen. You can see there what page you're on and your total page count and then right next to that is the total word count for the document. If you highlight a selection of text the word count will change to show X of Y words so that you can see the number of words in your selection (X) as well as the total number of words in the document (Y).

You can also click on the Word Count option in the Proofing section of the Review tab. This will immediately bring up the Word Count dialogue box:

As you can see, it gives a little more information than just word count (which is the second line of information). You also have the number of pages, the number of characters with and without spaces, the number of paragraphs, and the number of lines.

I use the characters option sometimes when I complete online forms that have a character limit but don't tell me how many characters I've used. I type my entry up in Word, check the character count, and then copy it over to the website.

Read Aloud

Just to the right of those three options in the Speech section of the Review tab is the Read Aloud option.

With this option, you can highlight a selection of text in your document, click on Read Aloud, and a computerized voice will read the text to you.

I find this a nice way to review the final draft of my fiction, although it sometimes has very interesting ideas of how to pronounce certain words. For example, grimaced.

Overall, though, it's a good trick to catch those last few straggling errors that the eye tends to skip right over.

(Although not all of them. You never catch them all. I used to write business reports that were reviewed by six people, three of whom were detailed-oriented lawyers who'd gone to schools like Yale and Harvard ,and it never failed that we'd give the client the report and then I'd see a typo that we'd all missed. On page one.)

Show/Hide Paragraph Marks

By default I do not show paragraph and other marks in my document, but when I'm trouble-shooting issues in a document this can be invaluable. The option to show or hide these marks is found in the Paragraph section of the Home tab and is in the top left corner. It looks like a paragraph mark. Click on it to turn on marks, click on it again to turn them off.

Once you turn on paragraph marks you'll be able to see indents, tabs, paragraph breaks, line breaks, section breaks, etc. Like in this example here:

If you look closely you should see a small dot between every single word. That indicates a space. Two dots in a row would indicate two spaces. At the end of every line that uses an Enter there is a paragraph mark. This example has two of those, one after "terminology." in the first line and one after "test" in the second line.

I've also included a tab which is indicated by the arrow on the second line before "test".

And there's a Section Break that will start the next line of text on the next page which is marked with a dashed line and text describing the type of break.

Showing paragraph marks is useful for finding those little annoyances like tabs or extra enters or a page or section break somewhere it wasn't supposed to be. You can often guess that they're there, but this is the only surefire way to know exactly what you're dealing with.

* * *

Alright, next we're going to cover some of the customized settings available under the Options section of the File tab.

File Options Customized Settings

Click on the File tab and then choose Options from the left-hand side and this will bring up the Word Options dialogue box which has a number of categories for options you can customize.

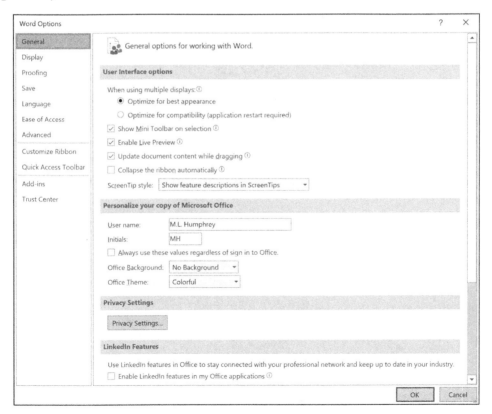

I'm not going to cover everything you can do here because there are easily over a hundred different settings, but I will point out some of the ones I've needed to use in the past.

General

The main change I've needed to make here is in the Personalize Your Copy of Microsoft Office section. As you can see in the screenshot above it defaults to showing my initials as MH, but I've in the past been on work teams where someone else had those same initials and that can be problematic for track changes. So this is where to adjust that to MLH for me, for example.

It also shows the ability to change the user name, but I want to say that I had to go into BIOS or somewhere to actually change my name to my initials for Office. So you can try it here, but it may not work or it may not hold for anything other than track changes. Be sure to check the box that says to always use those values regardless of sign in to Office, but then be careful if you have multiple users on the same computer.

(Basically, if this matters for you, double-check that it's working properly before you send the document off or take screenshots.)

Display

It looks like it's the default in Word 2019, but I always make sure that it says show white space between pages in print layout view. Without this box checked, you can't visually see page breaks in your document, one page of text rolls right into the next with just a thin gray line to indicate a page break.

That's especially annoying if you're working with a document that has very short sections that are supposed to fall on their own page because you can end up with three or four of them displayed on a single page.

I never customize the section that asks to show formatting marks on the screen because I only turn that on when I need that as discussed above, otherwise I want them hidden. But if find that you have marks showing in a document that won't turn off, check here to see if someone changed the settings so that some marks would be permanently visible.

Proofing

The Proofing section allows you to control when Word applies its AutoCorrect options and which ones it applies.

This one I always make changes to. (I haven't yet on this version of Word because I wanted to write this book first and it's driving me crazy to deal with the defaults.)

AutoCorrect Options

Most of the changes I make in this section are under the AutoCorrect Options. I click on that button and it brings up the AutoCorrect dialogue box which has five available tabs. I use the AutoCorrect, AutoFormat as You Type, and AutoFormat tabs to make adjustments.

For example, at my old job on the AutoCorrect tab I would always delete that first option to change (c) into the copyright sign because my job involved a lot of rule citations, where you write things like Rule 3070(c) which made it really annoying each time Word automatically changed that over to a copyright sign.

Your other option is to use Ctrl + Z when Word makes a correction you don't want. (My problem is that I'm usually about three words past the change before

I realize what's happened. At that point it becomes more of a hassle than it's worth.)

The AutoFormat As You Type and AutoFormat tabs include the setting for smart quotes versus straight quotes, which is another one I often change.

Smart quotes curve towards the text and are what you're supposed to use for dialogue, for example. But straight quotes are what you need to use in Excel formulas. So when I'm writing my Excel books I usually turn this one off.

It actually needs to be turned off in both of those tabs for it to work properly.

I will also sometimes turn off the setting that converts a fraction and the one that automatically creates hyperlinks, depending on what I'm working on.

Now, don't get me wrong. A lot of the autocorrect options are very handy—I often type too fast and mistype "the" as "teh" and Word always catches that for me—but do keep an eye out for "errors" you don't want fixed as you type like turning a single i into a capital I.

The AutoCorrect dialogue box is also where you can see that Word will automatically convert two dashes in a row into an em-dash.

(But only after you type a word, two dashes, another word, and a space.)

This is also where you can see that three periods in a row will turn into an ellipsis which treats them as one single character and keeps them together.

If you like to learn shortcuts or ways to make life easier that it's probably worth looking through these tabs to know what Word will do on your behalf so you can leverage it.

But if you're more like me then you'll probably wait to look at this section until you get annoyed with something that keeps happening that you want to turn off.

Check Spelling As You Type

In the third section of the Proofing screen you can uncheck the box that says to check spelling as you type so that you no longer have to see those red squiggly lines under words.

Mark Grammar Errors As You Type

Same for grammar errors. You can uncheck the box for that option to turn that off so that you aren't seeing the blue double underline in your document as you type.

This is also the section for turning off the grammar check altogether. Uncheck Check Grammar With Spelling and Word will no longer check for grammar when you select the Spelling and Grammar option on the Review tab.

Reset Spelling and Grammar Check

As mentioned previously, you can click on Recheck Document to reset the spelling and grammar check for the document. If you checked the document previously and told it to ignore errors but want to see those errors now, this is the way to do that.

Save

Prior to Word 2019 I would have recommended saving documents as a .doc instead of the default format which is .docx to ensure backward compatibility. Versions of Word from 2007 onward use .docx as their default but it's a format that users of Word versions prior to that can't open.

We're probably now in the safe range where most users have upgraded to new enough versions of Word that this isn't a concern. But if it ever is and you don't want to have to think about it you can change the default file format that Word uses to save your documents here.

This is also where you can specify how often Word saves an AutoRecovery version of your file. The default is set to 10 minutes. If you're ever working in Word and it crashes on you, then when you reopen that file in Word it will offer to let you open the recovery version instead which by default was saved at some point in the last ten minutes.

Word does not crash on me often, but when it does this has been a lifesaver for me. (More often it's that my entire computer crashed on me, not just Word.)

Normally the AutoRecovery process is so seamless you won't even notice it's happening, but I do have a set of formatted templates I work with that for some reason take long enough to save that they will freeze my computer for a minute or so as they save. Having that happen every ten minutes can be annoying, to say the least, so when working with them I will sometimes adjust this setting.

This section also lets you choose your default location for saving files, so if you always want to save to an X drive or something, this is where to change that setting.

Advanced

There are many options in this section. I can see a few that might be useful to change, like unchecking the allow text to be dragged and dropped option since I don't do that intentionally but have had it happen a few times unintentionally.

This is also the section where if you're going to work with documents that need high resolution images for print you'll want to change the default. Otherwise all of your images, no matter what their quality is when you bring them into Word will be 220 dpi which is generally considered too low for printing standards.

Customize Ribbon

The Customize Ribbon option lets you choose which tasks are available at the top of the screen in your Word workspace. So, for example, the options under the Home tab.

I would advise against this unless you work for yourself and have no expectation that you will ever use anyone else's computer or any public computer. Because what makes things faster for you in your version will significantly slow you down on anyone else's computer.

Also, you'll have to do this again with any new version of Word you buy which means another significant slowdown every couple of years as you upgrade to a new software version.

Not to mention, if you get stuck no one else will have the display you do so you'll be on your own trying to figure out where something is.

Quick Access Toolbar

Customizing the Quick Access Toolbar, on the other hand, makes a lot of sense if there are just one or two tasks that you use often that are located in a tab other than the one you usually need.

For me, for example, I usually put Breaks and Format Painter here so that I can access those from wherever I am.

File Info

We just discussed the File Options choices, but there's another section of the File tab that I want to explore and that's the Info section.

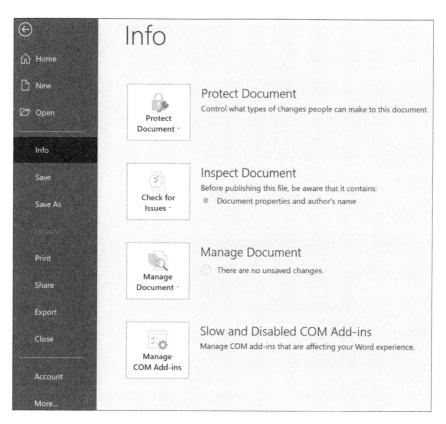

You reach it by clicking on the File tab and then the Info option on the left-hand side of the screen.

One of the things you can do here is strip the document of any personal information. So the author name, any track changes, any comments, etc. There are definitely times this is called for and you should always check a document for track changes before you hand it off to a client or professor or some other person who wasn't meant to see your comments and changes.

(I've been on the receiving end a few times of documents where that didn't happen and let's just say that you don't want to give you regulator the track changes version of your response to their inquiry...)

Which means it's a useful and necessary thing to be able to do. BUT. I hesitate to tell you about it because when used at the wrong time it can be a disaster. I have had people strip out the author information on a working document and then every single person's comments were listed as "Author" even if those comments were added after that point in time. So be careful with this, please.

Okay. The way you review a document for information you might want to remove is by clicking on the Check for Issues box next to where it says Inspect Document. From that dropdown then choose Inspect Document.

(You can see that this also gives you the option to Check Compatibility with older versions of Word, too, should that ever be an issue.)

When you choose to inspect the document Word will prompt you to save it if you haven't already and will then give you a list of categories it can scan for:

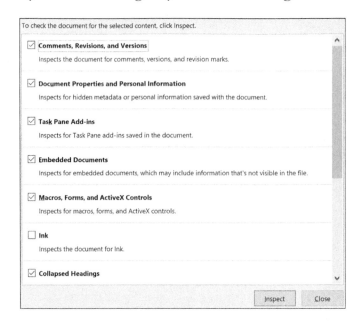

I usually scan for everything. When the scan is done it will display another dialogue box with any issues it found and let you choose which issues to fix:

BE VERY CAREFUL at this point that you don't remove something you will need and can't get back. (Like author information in a working document.)

What I recommend is that you save a copy of the file before you inspect it and then save the inspected and stripped down version as a new file. That way if you did delete something you shouldn't, you can go back and fix it.

That's basically all I use this section for, but as I mentioned above you can check for compatibility with older versions of Word.

You can also protect the document so that people can't edit it and password protect the document so that no one can open unless they have the password. (Just be sure you remember your password or you won't be able to open the file either.)

Okay. Now we're up to printing a document. But before we can print we need to know how to format the page so that it has page numbers and headers and footers. So let's cover that next.

Page Formatting

If you're going to print a document that is more than one page long, chances are you'll want to add page numbering to the document as well as maybe a header or footer that includes the document title or your name or both. Let's talk about how to do that.

Page Numbering

First, do not ever manually number your pages. Word will do this for you. By letting Word do this, you ensure that the page numbering will still work even when you make edits to the document.

Nothing worse than putting a 1 at the bottom of what you think is page one and then deciding to add a title to the document and suddenly there's a random 1 in the middle of the second page.

So don't do that. Please.

(Says the person who has occasionally been stuck fixing a document where someone did in fact do this. That and the person who manually formatted the text to *look* like track changes...Took me ages to realize what that person had done. And even longer to fix it. But you're reading this book so you won't do that kind of thing, right? Right.)

To add page numbers to your document, go to the Header & Footer section of the Insert tab which is towards the right-hand side, and click on the arrow next to Page Number.

This will bring up a dropdown menu that lets you choose where on the page you want your page numbers to display. If you hold your mouse over those options, you can then choose how you want those page numbers to look.

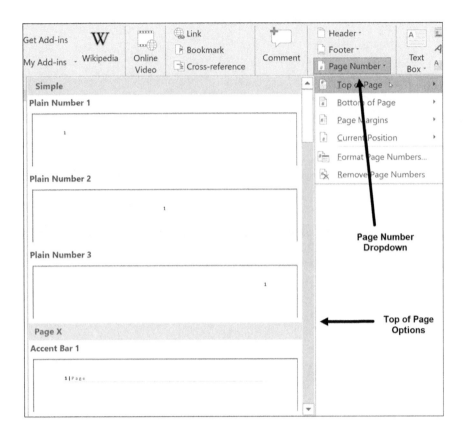

Above I've held my mouse over Top of Page and you can see the first four options I have to choose from, left, middle, right, and a left-hand accented option. If I scroll down in that list there are actually twenty-five total options to choose from some of which are quite distinctive.

Click on the choice you want and Word will insert it into the header (for top of page) or footer (for bottom of page). If you choose the page margins options, that is inserted into a standalone text box on the side of the page.

Current Position will insert the page number where your cursor currently is, so I'd only use that one if you already have a header or footer in your document (or a text box you want to use) and you're clicked into that space.

The Format Page Number option in that dropdown can be used to change the numbering format (to small case Roman numerals for example), the starting page number, or to specify that the numbering should or should not continue from a prior section. (This becomes much more relevant when you have sections in your document that require separate numbering. I cover how to create sections in *Word 2019 Intermediate*.)

For a basic simple page number using the dropdown menu and choosing one of the defaults should really be all you have to do.

Headers and Footers

Inserting a page number is basically a specialized version of inserting a header or footer. When you insert the page number at the top of the page or the bottom of the page Word creates a space that is separate from your main text and puts the page number there. But you can also put other text into the header or footer like your name or the title of the document.

Doing so will repeat that text at the top or bottom of the page for the entire document. (Or section if you're using sections. Also, you can set it up so that alternating pages have different text in them like a book does. But for basic headers and footers it repeats throughout the document.)

A header goes at the top of your page.

A footer goes at the bottom of your page.

To add one, go to the Header & Footer section of the Insert tab and click on the arrow below the one you need (header or footer), and then choose the option that works best for you, just like you did with page numbering.

Just like with page numbering you will have various pre-formatted options to choose from like these three for the footer:

You're not stuck with the format you choose. For example, with short story submissions, they usually want the header to be in the top right corner. If you choose the Blank header option, that creates a header that's in the top left corner. But you can simply go to the Home tab and choose to right-align the text in your header and that will put it in the right corner instead.

After you choose your header or footer option, Word creates a header or footer and inserts [Type here] into the designated spots where you're supposed to put text.

To edit that text, just start typing because it will already be highlighted in gray. If it isn't highlighted in gray, select the text and then start typing.

Text in your header or footer works just like text in your document. You can use the same options from the Home tab to change your font, font size, color, etc.

As mentioned above, headers and footers are in a separate area from the main text of your document. If you're in a header or footer and want to go back to the main document, you can (1) double-click back onto the main body of your document, (2) click on Close Header and Footer in the menu bar which should be showing in the Design tab under Header & Footer Tools, or (3) hit the Esc key on your keyboard.

If you're in your main document and want to edit your header or footer, you can (1) double-click on the text in the header or footer, or (2) right-click on the header or footer and choose "Edit Header" or "Edit Footer" from the dropdown.

Margins

Margins are the white space along the edges of your document. The default margins in Word 2019 are one-inch margins all around which is pretty standard so you probably won't have to edit this often.

But if you need to edit your margins, you can go to the Layout tab and under the Page Setup section click on the dropdown under Margins. This will give you the choice of Normal, Narrow, Moderate, Wide, Mirrored, Office 2003 Default, and Custom Margins.

Mirrored margins are for printed texts where the inside margins are the same for facing pages and the outside margins are the same for facing pages. (As opposed to thinking about the left-hand margin and the right-hand margin which is what you think about with a report or other printed document that is seen one single page at a time.)

Each option, except Custom Margins, shows what the margins are for that option.

Clicking on Custom Margins, will open the Page Setup dialogue box directly onto the Margins tab. You can also open the Page Setup dialogue box to the Margins tab by clicking on the expansion arrow for the Page Setup section.

This lets you specify a custom value for each margin as well as for the document gutter. (Which matters if you're printing book-style.) In the Pages section dropdown you can also specify that the margins should be mirrored.

Page Orientation

A standard document has a page orientation of portrait. That's where the long edge of the document is along the sides and the short edge is across the bottom and top. This is how most books, business reports, and school papers are formatted, and it's the default in Word.

But sometimes you'll create a document where you need to turn the text ninety degrees so that the long edge is at the top and bottom and the short edge is on the sides.

A lot of tables in appendixes are done this way. Also presentation slides are often this way. That's called landscape orientation.

(Think paintings here. A drawing of a person—a portrait—is generally taller than it is wide. A drawing of a mountain range—a landscape—is generally wider than it is tall.)

To change the orientation of your document, go to the Page Setup section of the Layout tab, click on the arrow under Orientation, and choose the orientation you want.

If you use section breaks--which are covered in *Word 2019 Intermediate*—you can set the page orientation on a section-by-section basis. But if you're not using sections, changing the orientation on any page will change the orientation of the entire document so be careful with this one.

You can also change the orientation in the Page Setup dialogue box which can be opened via the expansion arrow for the Page Setup section. The orientation option is on the Margins tab directly below the Margins settings.

Printing

Printing in Word, at its most basic, is incredibly easy. You can simply type Ctrl + P or go to File and choose Print from the list of options on the left-hand side. Both options will bring you to the Print screen.

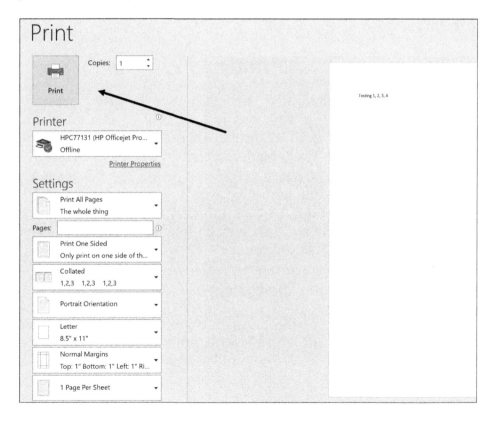

If all you want is to print the document with no adjustments, click on the printer image (see screenshot above) that's directly below where it says Print.

A lot of times this should be fine. It's not like Excel where you really need to check what it's going to look like because in Word as you were working you could see what it was going to look like.

But just in case, on the right-hand side Word will show you a preview of what the document will look like when it prints. For documents that are longer than a page, you can use the arrows at the bottom to navigate through the document preview.

There are a number of adjustments you can make before you print that will impact what prints and how.

Let's walk through those now from top to bottom.

Copies

Right next to the Print icon you can specify the number of copies you want to print. The default is one copy. To increase that amount, either click into the box and type a new number or use the arrows on the right-hand side to increase or decrease the number.

Printer

Your default printer should already be showing under the printer option.

Sometimes I don't want to print a physical copy of a document and so I'll choose the Microsoft Print to PDF or the Microsoft XPS Document Writer option instead of my printer. This creates a version of the document I can save to my computer.

There are a few other options there that I don't use, but you may, like fax.

If you do change your printer at some point, be sure to change it back next time you go to print. I usually realize I haven't when instead of printing Word asks me where I want to save the document.

Settings

Below the printer choice are all the Settings options that let you choose what portions of the document to print and how to print them.

Print All Pages Or Other Page Selections

The first choice you have is what portion of the document to print. The default is Print All Pages which will print the entire document.

If you click on that dropdown, however, there are a number of other choices. Print Selection will print any text that you have selected in the document.

Print Current Page will print the page you were clicked onto when you chose to print. You can verify that it's the right page in the print preview to the right.

Custom Print uses the pages box directly below the dropdown. You can type in the specific pages you want there. For page ranges, use a dash. For a list of individual pages, use commas.

So if you want to print pages 3, 5, and 7 you would enter "3,5,7" in the Pages box. If you wanted to print pages 3 through 7, you would enter "3-7" in the box.

If you go directly to the pages box and start typing in a page range it will automatically change the dropdown to "Custom Print."

You can also print in Word 2019 the Document Info, List of Markup which is your tracked changes, a list of the styles being used in the document, a list of items in your autotext gallery, and a list of any custom shortcut keys you have.

You can also choose to print only odd pages or only even pages.

And there's a choice to print the document with markup.

Print One-Sided or Two-Sided

The default is for Word to print on one side of the page, but you can change it to print two-sided documents.

To do so, click on the arrow next to the default choice of one-sided. You'll now see a dropdown with four options, one-sided, both sides with the long edge, both sides with the short edge, and manually print on both sides.

Choose the manual option if you have a printer that isn't set up to print two-sided documents automatically.

Choose to flip pages on the long edge for documents with a portrait orientation. Choose to flip pages on the short edge for documents with a landscape orientation.

Collation

This is only relevant if you're printing more than one copy of a document that's more than one page long.

The default when printing multiple copies of a document is to print one entire copy of the document and then print the next copy of the document. (That's the *collated* option that shows 1,2,3 1,23 1,2,3.)

The other option you can choose is to print all of your page ones and then all of your page twos and then all of your page threes. (That's the *uncollated* option that shows 1,1,1 2,2,2, 3,3,3)

The uncollated option is useful for situations where you might be giving out handouts one page at a time, but generally you'll want to stick with collated copies.

Orientation

We talked about this one before, but if you want the text on your page to go across the long edge instead of across the short edge, this is another place where you can make that choice.

The default is Portrait Orientation, but if you click on the arrow, you can instead choose Landscape Orientation.

Paper Size

The default in Word (at least in the U.S. version) is to print on 8.5"x11" paper. If you want to print your document on a different size of paper (say A4 or legal), then this is where you'd change that setting.

There are an insane number of choices both on the dropdown menu and if you click on More Paper Sizes, but for most documents you'll probably be using the default.

Make sure you have whatever paper you end up choosing if you're printing to an actual printer.

Margins

We already talked about how to change the margins on your document, but this is also another place where you can do that. You have the same pre-formatted margin choices here as in the Layout tab as well as the custom option.

Pages To Print Per Sheet

If you want to save paper because perhaps you're reviewing a document and it's not the final version, you can print more than one page of your document onto a single sheet.

The default is to print one page on one sheet, but if you click on the dropdown menu you can choose to print 2, 4, 6, 8, or 16 pages per sheet.

You can also choose to scale your text to a chosen paper size.

Be careful with this setting because Word will let you make a choice that results in an illegible document. Four pages on one page is still legible, but I suspect that sixteen pages on one page would be a challenge for most people to read. (But it may be useful if you're ever in a situation where your teacher said you could bring one page of notes and you're trying to cram an entire semester's worth of knowledge on that one page...)

Page Setup

As a beginner, I'd ignore the Page Setup link at the bottom of the page. Most of what it covers we've already addressed above. It's just the older way of specifying your print settings.

Conclusion

Alright. There you have it. Enough knowledge about Word to let you do most of what you need to do on a daily basis.

If you want to learn more, in *Word 2019 Intermediate* I dive into how to create complex numbered lists, insert tables, use section breaks, insert a table of contents, use styles, add watermarks and hyperlinks, deal with track changes, and more. Things that you may need to do at some point, but aren't essential to get started with Word.

You don't have to continue with that book, though. Word also has excellent help available.

The first option is to hold your mouse over any of the options in the menu at the top, like here for Format Painter. This will give you a basic description of what the option does as well as list any control shortcut that exists for it.

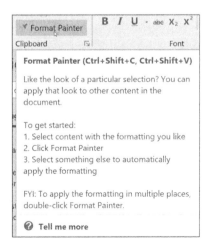

Many of the options will include Tell Me More at the bottom. You can click on that and it will open the Help task pane to a help pane specific to that topic.

You can also click on Help under the Help tab. This will open the Help task pane as well but to a generic starter screen where you can then browse the subject categories or search for what you're trying to do.

The Help tab also has a Show Training option which brings up a list of topics where you can then watch videos on each of the listed topics which can be helpful in learning something new.

If none of that works I will often do an internet search for what I'm looking for using "microsoft word" as part of my search string. So I might search for "how to add a hyperlink microsoft word." I then choose the support.microsoft. com option.

That's an excellent resource for how things work, but sometimes I need "is this possible" help, in which case I'll look to user forums to see if anyone else has asked my question before. (I find I need this less with Word than with Excel, though.)

You can also email me at mlhumphreywriter@gmail.com. I'm happy to point you in the right direction or figure out the answer myself and share it if I don't already know it. Sometimes it's just a matter of knowing the right buzz words to use to ask the question.

Okay. So that's it. Good luck with it! Don't let it scare you. If you're nervous then save drafts of what you're working on so you can go back to a prior version that was working for you. But generally just take it slow and easy and you should be fine. Especially if you stick to the basics we covered here.

Word 2019 Intermediate

WORD ESSENTIALS 2019 BOOK 2

M.L. HUMPHREY

CONTENTS

CONTENTS (CONT.)

Introduction

In *Word 2019 Beginner* we walked through the basics of what you need to know in order to use Word 2019 on a day-to-day basis, including how to open a file, how to enter text, how to format that text as well as your paragraphs and your document overall, customizing Word to meet your needs, and printing and saving your document.

But there's a lot more you can do in Word.

If you use Word in a business setting, chances are you'll also want to know how to create and format a table, insert images into your document, have Word create a table of contents for you, use Styles, track changes, insert comments, and use section and page breaks to allow for different page formatting in the same document.

We're going to cover all of that as well as some fairly simple things you can do in Word, like add hyperlinks, watermarks, and numbered lines to your document.

There are still some aspects of Word I'm not going to cover in this guide, mostly design-based functions like creating SmartArt or using WordArt. But by the time you're done with this guide you should be comfortable enough in Word to explore those on your own if you need to. In my experience, all of the Office products follow a certain predictable logic that you can apply to any task once you know enough about how the programs are structured.

Also, this guide is focused on Word 2019. Unlike in *Intermediate Word*, its predecessor which was written using Word 2013, I am not going to point out potential differences between this version of Word and others, nor am I going to work in Compatibility Mode.

I'm going to just focus on how things work in Word 2019 and not worry about what you could or could not do in older versions of Word.

But do know that if you are working with others who use versions of Word prior to 2007 they will only be able to open .doc documents and not the Word 2019 default which is a .docx document.

(We're getting to the point where that's now less of an issue, but it may still come up. If it does, you can always Save As to the older version, but you may lose some bells and whistles and functionality so be aware of this issue. The fancier you make your document, the more likely you are to have a problem.

Alright then. Let's get started by reviewing some basic terminology which was covered in detail in *Word 2019 Beginner.*

Basic Terminology

Below are some basic terms that I'll use throughout this guide. I want to make sure that you're familiar with them before we start.

Tab

I refer to the menu choices at the top of the screen (File, Home, Insert, Design, Layout, References, Mailings, Review, View, and Help) as tabs.

Click

If I tell you to click on something, that means to use your mouse (or trackpad) to move the arrow on the screen over to a specific location and left-click or right-click on the option. If I don't specify which to use, left-click.

Select or Highlight

If I tell you to select text, that means to highlight that text either by using your mouse or the arrow and shift keys. Selected text is highlighted in gray.

Dropdown Menu

A dropdown menu provides you a list of choices to select from. There are dropdown menus when you right-click in your document workspace as well as for some of the options listed under the tabs at the top of the screen. Each option with a small arrow next to it will have a dropdown menu available.

Expansion Arrows

I refer to the little arrows at the bottom right corner of most of the sections in each tab as expansion arrows. For example, click on the expansion arrow in the Clipboard section of the Home tab and it will open the Clipboard task pane.

Dialogue Box

Dialogue boxes are pop-up boxes that cover specialized settings. They allow the most granular level of control over an option.

Scroll Bar

Scroll bars are on the right-hand side of the workspace and sometimes along the bottom. They allow you to scroll through your document if your text takes up more space than you can see in the workspace.

Arrow

If I ever tell you to arrow to the left or right or up or down, that just means use your arrow keys.

Task Pane

I refer to the panes that sometimes appear to the left, right, and bottom of the main workspace as task panes. By default you should see the Navigation task pane on the left-hand side when you open a new document in Word.

Control Shortcut

I'll occasionally mention control shortcuts that you can use to perform tasks. When I reference them I'll do so by writing it as Ctrl + a capital letter. For example, Save is Ctrl + S.

To use one, hold down the Ctrl key and the letter at the same time.

Styles

Let's dive right in with one of the most valuable tools in Word. (Maybe right after the Format Painter that was discussed in *Word 2019 Beginner*.) And that's Styles.

Styles let you set the formatting for a paragraph once and then apply that formatting to other paragraphs with a simple click. I wrote and formatted *Intermediate Word*, the precursor to this book, in Word and I was able to format the entire book using three styles, one for the chapter headings, one for the first paragraph of a section or chapter, and one for every other paragraph.

Rather than having to remember that I'd indented the paragraph by X amount and had Y line spacing and that it was justified and what the font and font size were, I could just establish that "first paragraph" or "body text" style and then forget about all those settings for the rest of the document.

(For the curious I'm formatting this particular book using a product called Affinity Publisher which also uses styles, but is not Word.)

Okay, so how do you work with styles?

Word by default uses a style called Normal. In my version of Word 2019 that style uses the Calibri font in an 11 point size with left-aligned paragraphs, a line spacing of 1.08, and a space of 8 points after each paragraph. It also includes widow and orphan control meaning that there will not be a single line left alone at the top or bottom of a page if that line is part of a paragraph.

You can see this by looking at the Styles section of the Home tab where the Normal style has a box around it to show that's the current style in use.

To see the current settings for a style, you can right-click and choose Modify from the dropdown menu.

Here you can see that the Normal style is selected and the Modify option is the second in the dropdown menu.

Clicking on Modify will bring up the Modify Style dialogue box which has all of the current settings for that style. We'll look at one of those in a moment.

In the meantime, this is what the Normal style looks like in a document:

This is a test paragraph so we can see what the Normal paragraph style looks like and how it works when there is more than one line of text. As you can see it left-justifies the text, there is no indent and there is a decent amount of space between lines.

When you start a new paragraph there is a space between the two paragraphs. All of this is part of the Normal style.

I often will write a document using the default style, but I almost never want that style in my final version. (For most non-fiction and fiction the preferred format is to have the paragraphs touching one another and to signal the beginning of a new paragraph by using an indent.)

In addition to the Normal style, Word also provides a number of other preformatted styles such as headings, title format, subtitle, emphasis, etc. Each one is formatted in the style section like it will be in the document.

My list of styles displays on two rows. Here is the first row of choices I see with Normal having a gray box that indicates it's the current style in use.

(The number of visible styles may differ for you depending on the zoom level of your screen.)

To see all of the available styles, use the arrows on the right-hand side to move up or down one row of choices at a time.

You can see what each one will look like in your document by holding your mouse over it. When you do that, the paragraph you're currently clicked into will briefly change to show the style.

An obvious example to try this with is the Intense Quote option which colors the text blue, centers it, and puts lines above and below the paragraph.

Here I've gone ahead and applied that style to a paragraph:

To apply a style, click somewhere on the paragraph you want to format (you don't even have to highlight the whole thing if it's just one paragraph), and then click on the style you want to use.

It's as easy as that.

If you want to see all styles at once, clicking on the down-pointing arrow with a line above it on the right-hand side of the visible styles. That will also give you the Create a Style, Clear Formatting, and Apply Styles choices.

Another point to make about the pre-formatted styles is that using the heading styles (Heading 1, Heading 2, etc.) will also create navigation options that you can use to move throughout your document as well as rearrange your document.

If you have the Navigation pane open (which you can do using Ctrl + F for Find if it isn't already open), click on Headings and you'll see a listing of every text entry that is formatted with one of the heading styles. For example, here I've formatted Introduction and Basic Terminology with the Heading 1 style:

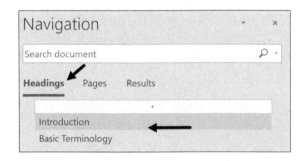

You can click on any of the entries in the Headings section to be taken to that point in the document. You can also click and drag a heading name in that section to a new position in the list and Word will move all of the text for that section to that new location in the document.

(Although be careful with that click and drag option if you're working in a heavily-formatted document. I just did that with the above two sections, clicking and dragging Introduction to after Basic Terminology. Because the document was a hundred-plus pages long and the other chapters weren't formatted using Heading 1, it put the Introduction chapter starting on the same page as the last chapter and with page numbering of 1, 2, 3 even though it was immediately after page 245. Also, because the Basic Terminology chapter was set to continue page numbering, even though it was now the first chapter it was numbered starting at page 11 because of the front matter in the document.)

Okay, so that's how the default styles work. To apply one, highlight the text or click on the paragraph you want to format, go to the Styles section of the Home tab, and click on the style you want.

But the real power comes from creating your own styles.

It only takes setting a style up once and then you can apply that style in all of your documents going forward to create a consistent appearance both within the document in question and across all of your documents.

The easiest way to do this is if there's a style you already like in another document you can use the Format Painter to copy it to a new document. Just highlight a paragraph with the style you want in the first document, click on Format Painter, and then click on a paragraph in the second document to apply the style.

Not only will that paragraph change to that style, but the style will also be added to your list of available styles in the Styles section of the Home tab, which means you can easily apply that style to the rest of the document.

Let's walk through an example of how to apply that style to the rest of the document. Say half of the paragraphs in your existing document are formatted in Awesome Style and you've brought in Even Better Style and applied it to a single paragraph, and now you want to apply it to all of the other paragraphs with Awesome Style.

You do not have to do this individually. You can select all of the paragraphs that are in Awesome Style by right-clicking on Awesome Style from the Home tab and choosing Select All X Instances from the dropdown menu where X is the number of paragraphs in that style in the document. Like here where I have 957 paragraphs in Awesome Style:

Once you've done that and all paragraphs in that style have been selected, you can simply click on the style you want to apply (Even Better Style in this case) and Word will apply that style to all of those paragraphs.

It takes less than a minute. Although with a big document like I was using here, give it just a few seconds to select all of the paragraphs and then a few more to apply the new style.

(And, no, I don't normally name my styles things like Awesome Style. I just did it for this example using the Rename option you see there in the dropdown.)

So that's one way to apply a new format in your document. Copy it from elsewhere.

But what if you don't have a style to copy? The easiest way to create a custom style is to take one paragraph and format it exactly how you want it. Choose your paragraph spacing, text alignment, font, font size, etc.

Once that's ready, go to the Styles section of the Home tab and at the end of the box that shows the available styles, click on that arrow with a line above it that we talked about earlier to expand the section until you can see the Create a Style option. Click on that and give your style a name.

If you need to make further modifications to the formatting of your new style, right-click on the style name, choose Modify to bring up the Modify Style dialogue box.

Another option for creating a new style is to click on the expansion arrow for the Styles section. This will bring up the Styles dialogue box. The bottom left image in that dialogue box is for New Style.

Clicking on that image will then bring up the Create New Style from Formatting dialogue box.

Basic formatting choices are available on that main screen, but you can also use the Format dropdown list in the bottom left corner to access more dialogue boxes with additional options for Font, Paragraph, Tabs, Border, Language, Frame, and Numbering options as well as a Shortcut Key dialogue box.

The Shortcut key option lets you assign a key sequence to use in your document to apply a format to your paragraph without having to click into the Styles section of the Home tab.

I've found that this can be a significant time saver if I am typing a document with alternating styles, such as this one. Not having to move from the keyboard to my mouse or trackpad saves considerable time.

Just give some thought to your shortcut combo so that it's easy to type. Also, when you add your shortcut Word will tell you if that's already in use or not. Like here where I tried to use Ctrl + Q and it was already listed as in use for some other purpose.

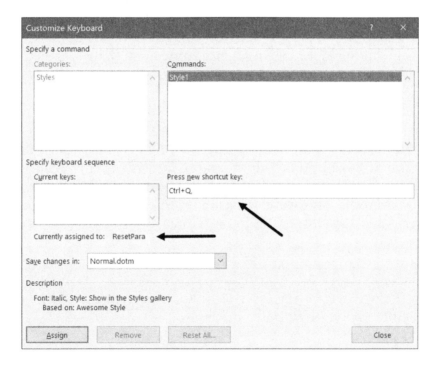

What about an existing style? What if it's close, but not quite where you want it? You can take one instance of that style in your document, format it exactly how you want it, and then go to that style in the Styles section of the Home tab, right-click and choose Update Style to Match Selection from the dropdown.

This will change all instances of that style in your document to the formatting you just used on that one paragraph.

A few more thoughts.

I never edit the Normal style. I don't think it's a good practice to do so, especially since by default your new styles will link to it and so any edit you make to that style will edit any linked styles.

Also, in the new style checkbox you can choose to either have the style you've created available in only that document or to make it available in all other Word documents. (I'm weird so I limit a style to the current document and then use Format Painter to transfer the style to a new document when it's needed. That let's me make sure I'm not having any unintended consequences like updating a style that another style relies upon and messing up some other document accidentally.)

The Manage Styles option, which is the third option in the Styles dialogue box, brings up a Manage Styles dialogue box. In the Set Defaults tab in that dialogue box you can change the default font and font size for Word.

In the Edit tab in that dialogue box you can see all styles that are available for use in Word, including many that do not appear in the Styles section of the Home tab. For example, the Footnote Text style does not appear in the Styles section of the Home tab but can be located and modified this way.

When creating a new style you do also have the option of basing it on an existing style. I've done this, for example, with a document where I have two paragraph styles that are identical except for one attribute, such as paragraph indent. That way when I update one of the styles the other one updates as well.

This can save a lot of time if you're changing the font or font size in a document, for example, and want to easily be able to do so across a number of related styles.

* * *

Alright, then. That's Styles. Incredibly useful once you master them, especially if you create custom styles. Now on to breaks.

Breaks

Breaks are another incredibly useful tool. They allow you control over a complex document so that you can specify exactly where each page should start, for example, as well as create different sections within a document that have different headers, footers, page numbering, page orientation, etc.

Never, and I repeat, never, should you use "Enter" in a document to get to the next page to start a new section or chapter. Do not do that. Use a page break instead.

Because think what happens if you change the font or font size or make edits in your document. Suddenly those ten enters you used are too many or too little and you end up with your Corporate Summary heading at the bottom of the page instead of the top where it belongs. And fixing that little issue may then lead to having to fix others.

Page breaks solve that issue and even as your text adjusts, they still do what they need to which is make sure that your next section starts where it should.

I have also worked at companies that created each section of a report as a separate document and then saved one final version of the whole thing as a merged PDF.

But that approach requires a lot of manual effort to keep the page numbering consistent across files, for example, and is much more prone to error. Far easier to use a section break to let Word know that this portion of a document is different in some crucial way from other sections of the document.

So. Page breaks and section breaks:

Learn them. Love them.

They are fantastic.

Basics

Breaks can be found in the Page Setup section of the Layout tab. If you click on the dropdown menu under Breaks, you'll see that there are multiple options to choose from.

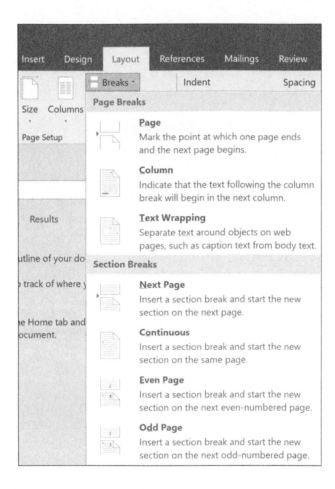

The two main sections are for Page Breaks and Section Breaks, which we'll define in a moment.

You can also insert a basic page break via the Pages section of the Insert tab or by using Ctrl + Return.

Page Breaks

Let's start with page breaks. Page breaks insert a break in your document so that your text moves to the next page or column, as the case may be, regardless of how much space is left on the page.

Page

The first option under Page Breaks is Page. This option ends the text on the current page at the point where the break is inserted and continues that text at the top of the next page.

Before you insert a page break, be sure to position your cursor at the end of the text (or image as the case may be) right before where you want the break.

For me this is usually the end of the last line of the last paragraph on the page.

Then you can use either Ctrl + Return or go to one of the Page break menu options and insert your page break.

When you do this, Word will move everything past that point down so that the next line of text (or image) starts at the top of the next page.

A page break can be useful for when you don't need to edit the header, footer, or page numbering, but you do need whatever comes next to move to the next page. For example, a chapter start or section start in a report or document where the header and footer are going to remain the same throughout the document.

(Sometimes when I insert a break, Word will stretch out the last line of text in that last line of text as if trying to justify it. If that ever happens to you, just click at the end of the line and hit enter. It'll move the page break to the next line and fix the text back to your normal formatting.)

Column

Column breaks come into play when you have your text formatted into multiple columns (which we'll discuss later).

A column break allows you to make sure that text you want in a specific column appears in that column.

To insert a column break, click into the text in your document at the point where you want the new column to start and then choose the Column break option under Page Breaks.

All text from that point forward will move to the next column.

Section Breaks

Section breaks are essential for when you want to use a different header, footer, page numbering, page orientation, or number of columns between different portions of your document.

Section breaks are what I use for breaks between chapters in a book where I have a blank left-hand page before my chapter starts. I also use them in all books to separate my front matter from the main body of the document so that I can have the proper page numbering in my books.

Another use for them would be in a report where the header in each section of the report needs to be different. Or where an appendix needs to be formatted using landscape orientation.

There are four types: Next Page, Continuous, Even Page, and Odd Page.

Next Page

The Next Page section break will insert a break and start the next section on the next page. So it's basically like a page break except that you can make changes to the section and not have them carry through to the whole document. (We'll talk about intermediate-level use of headers and footers next and discuss there how to combine a section break with different headers, footers, or page numbers across sections.)

It works just like page breaks. Go to the last line of the last paragraph for the prior section and then choose Next Page from under Section Breaks in the Breaks dropdown menu of the Page Setup section of the Layout tab.

Word will move everything from that point forward to the next page and will label that as a separate section of the document.

A next page section break and a standard page break will look exactly the same until you make changes to the header, footer, or page formatting.

Continuous

A continuous section break will not move the text to the next page but will separate the text on that page into separate sections.

The only time I can think I would use this one is if I had multiple paragraphs of text that I want to be in multiple columns on the same page with other text either before or after it that I wanted in a single column.

With columns, which we'll discuss later, you can format a single paragraph to have multiple columns by selecting that specific text first. But if you want to apply columns to multiple paragraphs at once, the easiest way is to click into that section of your document and change the number of columns for the whole section at once.

Even Page/Odd Page

The final two options are the Even Page and Odd Page section break options. The Even Page option will split the document at the point of the section break and will start the next section at the top of the next even-numbered page. The Odd page option will split the document at the point of the section break and start the new section at the top of the next odd-numbered page.

Theoretically these are even better than the Next Page option for something like a report or a book where you want each section or chapter to start on the right-hand side of the page, especially the Odd Page option.

But do be careful with this one. In prior versions of Word it has worked inconsistently for me. I've tested it in Word 2019 and it seems to be fine, but definitely double-check your document to make sure that all of your sections do in fact start on the even-numbered or odd-numbered page as you specified.

(The last time this gave me problems my current Odd Page section break looked like it was working just fine, but when I looked back at other Odd Page section breaks I'd added they had reverted to plain Next Page section breaks.)

Remove a Page or Section Break

If you ever need to remove a page or section break, you can just go to the end of the first section and use the delete key or go to the beginning of the next section and backspace. I usually use the delete option.

You don't need to see your page or section break to do this, but if you want to see your page or section break, you can click on the paragraph mark on the top right of the Paragraph section of the Home tab to show all breaks in the document.

A page or section break on its own line will show as a dotted line or two dotted lines across the page with Page Break or Section Break in the middle of the dotted line.

Sometimes if a page or section break is on the last line of a paragraph and not on its own line it won't be visible even if you have paragraph marks set to show. It will just appear as a few small dots at the end of the line if the text in that line takes up too much of the space.

A continuous section break is similar except it will be labeled Section Break (Continuous). Same for a column break which is labeled Column Break.

You can usually identify breaks by the way the text behaves where the break has been inserted since the text will move to another page for no apparent reason. (Although someone using Enter multiple times can get the same effect, so be careful.)

Headers and Footers (Intermediate Version)

Now that we've covered breaks let's revisit the topic of headers and footers, particularly some more advanced options for using them.

As a refresher, to insert a header, footer, or page number, you can do so by going to the Insert tab and choosing Header, Footer, or Page Number from the Header & Footer section. Each option has a dropdown menu with a number of various style choices.

To access a header or footer that you've already inserted into your document, you can simply double-click on that space. If that doesn't work, you can also right-click on the space and choose Edit Header or Edit Footer as the case may be.

To exit a header or footer and return to the main text of your document, you can use Esc or double-click in the main space of the document.

* * *

Alright. Now that we've covered those basics, let's talk about some fancier ways to format headers and footers, starting with changing your settings so that the first page of your document has a different header, footer, or page number than the rest of the document. (Very useful for printed reports or short story submissions, for example.)

Different First Page Header/Footer/Page Number

If you open most books you'll see that there isn't a header on the first page of any chapter. It's blank. But then the rest of the chapter does have a header.

And if you have a report with a cover page, chances are you don't want a header on that cover page. So how do you do this? How do you set it so that your first page has a different header or footer than the rest of your pages?

First, insert a header. If you've already done that, open the header.

In the menu bar above your document you should see a Design tab at the end of the listed tabs with the label Header & Footer Tools above it. Like this:

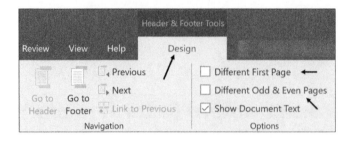

In the center of the choices under that tab is the Options section, pictured above on the right-hand side.

The first row of that section says Different First Page and has a checkbox. By default this option is not checked. But if you want a different first page header and/or footer for your document, you can check it.

Checking that box separates both the header *and* footer of the first page so that any edits made on that first page are exclusive to that page and any edits made in the header or footer in the rest of the document don't impact the first page.

Once you check that box you can delete the header on the first page and the header on all of the other pages will remain untouched, for example.

Since I generally want my footer on the first page to look the same as the rest of the document, I only check this box after I've finished all of my formatting. That ensures that the footers across my document are identical.

(I will add here that you shouldn't worry if it takes a few tries to get your headers and footers throughout your whole document looking the way you want them to. Especially when you start messing with different first page headers or, what we're about to talk about, different odd and even page headers. Also, different sections. I've been doing this for years and I still make mistakes. Remember Ctrl + Z (Undo) is your friend and there's not much that you can do wrong in Word that can't be fixed.)

Different Odd and Even Pages

Another choice you have in the Options section of the Header & Footer Tools Design tab is Different Odd & Even Pages.

I don't recall ever using this with a business report or school paper, but I use it for every single book I format. Pick up a book from your shelf and you should see that for every chapter the author name is on one page and the title or chapter name is on the opposite page. It's a rare book that's formatted differently than that.

So, how do you do this?

First, insert your header or footer.

Next, click on Different Odd & Even Pages in the Options section of the Header & Footer Tools Design tab.

Nothing will change immediately. Your header and footer will still look exactly like they did before, but now if you make a change to the header or footer ion an odd-numbered page it will only impact your other odd-numbered pages. Same for even-numbered pages.

(This all gets really fun when you have different headers and footers for first pages and then different headers and footers for odd and even pages because sometimes you have to go back three pages to find another page that has the same header and footer as the one you're working on.)

Headers and Footers and Section Breaks

The choices we just discussed allow for some pretty sophisticated formatting without ever requiring a section break. But if you have any blank pages in your document (say between chapters or sections) or if you need to have different headers or footers (say in an appendix or your front matter where you want a different page numbering or page numbering style), then you're going to need to combine the use of headers and footers with the use of section breaks.

The nice thing about Word is that it will default to continuing your page numbering when you insert a section break. This means that, for example, if you have multiple chapters in a document you don't have to worry about changing the page numbering settings every single chapter.

But there are going to be times that you do need to change your page numbering between sections. For example, between the table of contents in a report and the main content of the report.

Generally, you should use lower case Roman numerals (i, ii, iii, etc.) for the pages that contain the table of contents and use standard numbers (1, 2, 3, etc.) for the main body content. (Weirdly enough, you actually continue the standard numbers if you have any additional content at the back of the book and want to number those pages.)

Okay, so how do you do this?

I'm going to assume that you already have sections breaks in your document because this option is only available if there are already multiple sections.

The first step is to unlink one section from another. To do this, click into the header or footer of the first page where you want to see the change.

So if I have a table of contents and then the main body of a report, I'd go to the header or footer of the first page of that main body of the report.

If I have the main body of a report and then an appendix that I want to have a different header or footer, I'd go to the first page of the appendix.

Whichever one it is, you want the first page of the second section.

Once you've clicked into that header or footer, go to the Navigation section of the Headers & Footers Tools Design tab.

You'll see a Link to Previous option that is already selected by default.

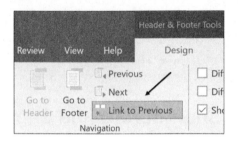

Click on it once to turn it off. It will no longer be highlighted in gray at that point.

Nothing will change when you do this. You will need to edit the header or footer in either or both of the two sections to see a difference.

Page Numbers and Section Breaks

For example, if you need to edit the page numbering of two sections like a table of contents and the main body of the document so that they have different page numbers, you'd need to make edits to the page numbering in both of those sections. In the main body you'd have to turn off the option to continue page numbering from the previous section and in the table of contents section you'd need to change the numbering format.

To change page numbering for a section, highlight a page number from that section, right-click, and choose Format Page Numbers from the dropdown menu. This will bring up the Page Number Format dialogue box. (Your other option is to go to the Header & Footer section of the Header & Footer Tools Design tab, click on the dropdown for Page Number, and choose Format Page Numbers from there. This too will bring up the Page Number Format dialogue box.)

At the top of the dialogue box you can change the style of the numbering. Your choices are 1, 2, 3 as well as i, ii, iii and then some stranger ones like a, b, c and I, II, III as well as one with dashes on either side of the 1, 2, 3.

At the bottom of the dialogue box you can uncheck the box to continue the page numbering from the previous section. The default will then be to start your page numbering for that section at 1 (or i or A, etc.).

You can also set a section to start at any number you want in the Start At field. So if for some reason you were using different Word files for different sections of a report (which you really shouldn't have to do) then you might set this value to 3, 5, or whatever the starting page number for the section needs to be.

So let's step back and look at that table of contents/main body example again and walk through the steps to create two separate sets of page numbers.

First, we'd go to the first page of the main body and unlink that section from the prior section.

Next, we could update the page numbering so that it does not continue from the previous section.

Finally, we could go to the table of contents section and change the number format for that section to i, ii, iii.

At that point all pages in the table of contents section should be numbered i, ii, iii etc. and all pages in the main body should be numbered 1, 2, 3, etc. with the main body section starting at page 1.

(And again, don't worry if you don't do this perfect the first time. I often forget one part or another and have to bounce back and forth between my various headers and footers to get things looking exactly how I want them to. Unless you do this all the time, it can be a bit of trial and error.)

Add Date And/Or Time To Your Header Or Footer

This one is actually pretty simple. To insert the date and/or time into your header or footer, go to the location where you want to insert it (the header or footer), and then go to the Header & Footer Tools Design tab.

(If your document doesn't already have a header or footer and this is all you want to insert, go to the Header & Footer section of the Insert tab, click on the dropdown for Header or Footer, and choose Edit Header or Edit Footer from the bottom of the dropdown. This will open a blank header or footer for you.)

In the Insert section of the Design tab, click on Date & Time. This will bring up a Date & Time dialogue box. Choose the date and/or time format you want and it will be inserted into your header or footer.

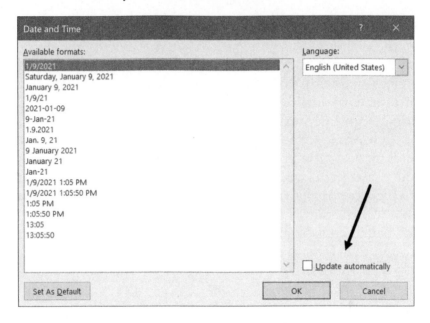

If you want the date and time to update so that it always displays the current date and/or time, be sure to check the box that says Update Automatically in the bottom right corner of the dialogue box.

(Just be sure that's what you really want. I can't count the number of memos I've seen where someone used the automatic date option and shouldn't have. Instead of the memo being dated the day it was actually written and finalized, the memo updated to the current date each time it was opened which can have serious ramifications under certain circumstances.)

Add Document Information or Photos To Your Header Or Footer

You can also have the header or footer include certain document information such as the Author, File Name, File Path, or Document Title.

It works just the same as adding a date or time except you use the Document Info dropdown in the Insert section of the Design tab.

You can choose Author, File Name, File Type, and Document Title from the dropdown menu. There is also a secondary dropdown menu for Document Property that includes fields like company information, publication date, and keywords.

If you want even more information choices, you can click on Field in the dropdown menu to bring up the Field dialogue box which includes a large number of additional fields you probably won't need. SectionPages does allow you to have Page X of Y for a section where Y is the SectionPages value. NumPages will do the same for the entire document.

All of the document information fields are dynamic fields, so will update as the information changes.

The Quick Parts dropdown next to that includes an AutoText option which appears to contain user name and user initials as two more default options.

The final two options in that Insert section are for pictures. This is helpful for if you ever need to include a logo in your header section. Just click on Pictures and then navigate to where your image is stored and select it.

The header or footer will expand to accommodate the image. Click on the round circle in the corner of the image and drag at an angle to resize it to the size you want.

You can also edit the dimensions of the photo in the Picture Tools Format tab that will appear when you insert a photo into the header or footer.

The Picture Tools Format tab also lets you adjust other image attributes. (We'll talk about those attributes more in the section on inserting images into a Word document, because they're the same whether you insert into a header or footer or into the main body of the document.)

Edit Header/Footer Position

By default in Word 2019, the header and footer are positioned .5" from the top and bottom of the page. If you want to change that setting, it's in the Position section of the Header & Footer Tools Design tab.

Edit Header/Footer Text Format

You can edit the formatting of the header or footer text just like you would any text in the main document. You can change the font, font size, font color, alignment, add bolding, italics, or underline, etc.

To do so, select the text you want to change and use the options in the mini formatting menu or the Font section of the Home tab.

You can also select the text you want to change and then right-click and choose Font to pull up the Font dialogue box which has two tabs in this instance, Font and Advanced. Font is for font choice, color, format, etc. Advanced is more for character spacing and things like that you probably won't use often.

You can also choose Paragraph from the dropdown menu to change indents, alignment, line spacing, etc. although, again, not one you're likely to use often.

Footnotes and Endnotes

Since we just talked about headers and footers, let's also talk about footnotes and endnotes.

Footnotes go at the bottom of the page. Endnotes go at the end of the document or the section. Other than that, they're pretty similar in how they work and how you insert them into your document.

To insert a footnote or endnote, click into the point in your main document text where you want to place the note and go to the Footnotes section of the References tab. Click on either Insert Footnote or Insert Endnote.

Word will then insert the footnote or endnote number at that point as a superscript number and will add a line either at the bottom of the page or the end of the document and put that same number below the line.

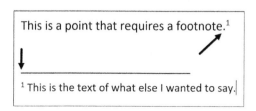

You can then type text next to the number at the bottom of the page or the end of the document like I did above.

The default in Word is for the footnote or endnote to be in 10 pt where the main text is in 11 pt.

If you want to change the font or font size in the note, I recommend updating the style associated with the note so that you only have to make that adjustment once.

To do so, right-click on the text in the note and choose Style from the dropdown menu. This will bring up a Style dialogue box that should have the name of the style already highlighted. Click on Modify to bring up a dialogue box where you can make your changes.

The Footnote and Endnote dialogue box allows for control over the placement of the notes as well as the numbering style for the notes. To access it, click on the expansion arrow in the Footnotes section of the References tab or right-click on the text of a note and choose Note options from the dropdown.

The Location section at the top of the dialogue box lets you determine where the endnote or footnote will be located.

For footnotes your choice is the bottom of the page or below the text. Choosing below the text means that if your text doesn't fill the entire page that the footnote will appear about a line below the text. Choosing bottom of the page means that even if there is only one line of text on a page the footnote will still be at the very bottom of the page.

For footnotes the choice is either to put the endnote at the end of the document or at the end of the section.

The Convert option allows you to turn footnotes into endnotes or endnotes into footnotes with one click. If your document has both you can also choose to swap them so that your footnotes become endnotes and your endnotes become footnotes.

Just click on Convert and then choose the option you want. (Remember that footnotes and endnotes have different styles applied to them if you do this so you may need to edit the style for the note type you're now using.)

The next section, Footnote Layout, lets you decide whether or not to display your footnotes in columns at the bottom of the page. I've seen this done a few times in lengthy non-fiction books with significant amounts of footnotes and small text in general. They kept the main body text in one column, but then had the footnotes in two columns to make it more clear which was which.

You can have up to four columns like I've done here where I also have notes showing below the text instead of at the end of the page.

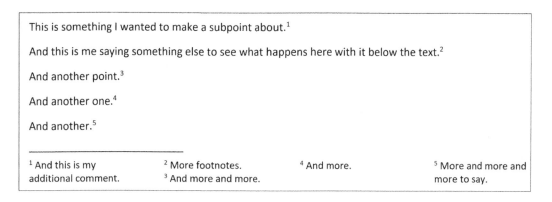

This is something I wanted to make a subpoint about.[1]

And this is me saying something else to see what happens here with it below the text.[2]

And another point.[3]

And another one.[4]

And another.[5]

[1] And this is my additional comment. [2] More footnotes. [3] And more and more. [4] And more. [5] More and more and more to say.

The Format section below that lets you choose the number format to use. Footnotes default to 1, 2, 3 and endnotes default to i, ii, iii but you can change that.

Custom mark lets you use marks instead of numbers. For example I've seen little daggers and other symbols used as footnote markers before. If you click on Symbol you can choose your desired symbol from the Symbol dialogue box.

When you click on your choice it will be inserted as a new footnote with the symbol you chose inserted at that point in your document as well as in the footnotes section.

The Start At option lets you dictate what number to start your footnotes or endnotes with.

The Numbering option lets you indicate if the numbering should be continuous throughout the document or restart with each section or page.

The final section lets you decide whether to apply your changes to the entire document or just the current section.

To navigate from one footnote or endnote to the next in your document, use the Next Footnote dropdown in the Footnotes section of the References tab.

The Show Notes option in the References tab will move you back and forth between a note and the position in the main body text where that note is used. (This can be very helpful when dealing with endnotes.)

You can also right-click on the text of a note and choose Go to Footnote or Go to Endnote to see the location of the note in the document.

To delete a footnote or endnote from your document, you have to do so in the document itself. Deleting the text of the footnote or endnote will still leave the number in your document. Only selecting and deleting the small superscripted number or symbol from within your main body text will delete the entire footnote or endnote.

Be careful applying styles to the main body text in a document that already has footnotes or endnotes. I tested this with a few different default styles provided by Word and some of them turned the superscript number or symbol used in the text to denote a footnote or endnote into normal text. It doesn't appear that changing the font size or font will do this in Word 2019, but changing the style sometimes did. Once that happened the only way to fix it was to Undo because changing the style back did not put the superscript formatting back.

With respect to track changes, if you have track changes turned on and you edit the text in a footnote or endnote, those edits will be shown in track changes. However, you cannot tie a comment to a footnote or endnote.

Also, when you're reading a document, if you want to see what the text of a footnote or endnote is without going to the actual note, you can do so by holding your cursor over the number in the text and it will appear as a note. But if you were working in track changes the text that appears is both the deleted and current text, as you can see in the example below.

Some Simple Tricks

Alright, that was a lot to dive right into, so let's step back and cover a few simple little tricks that I didn't cover in *Word 2019 Beginner*.

Links

If you want to add a link from your document to an outside source, whether that's a file or a website, or a link to another section of your existing document, you can do so with the link option.

Websites

The simplest and probably most common type of link is to a website.

One way to add one is to just copy the website address or type it into your document. For example, below I've done so with www.mlhumphrey.com.

You can find it at www.mlhumphrey.com.

Testing mlhumphrey.com

Once you do that Word will automatically convert the text to a hyperlink. It will turn blue and be underlined like in the first line above.

For a website address to be properly formatted as a link automatically it needs the www portion of the address, which is why the text on the second line was not turned into a link.

If you enter a website address and don't want it to be linked, then when Word converts it to a link just use Ctrl + Z to undo. You'll be left with the website address, but the link will be gone.

Of course, a lot of website addresses are long and ugly and you may not want to include the full address in your document. In that case, you can use any text in your document to create your link.

For example, I might write "You can access that website here" with a link tied to the word "here".

To do that, select the word or words you want to turn into a link and either go to the Links section of the Insert tab and click on Link or right-click on the text you've selected and choose Link from the dropdown menu.

Either option will bring up the Insert Hyperlink dialogue box.

The default choice on the left-hand side will be Existing File or Web Page. The text you selected will be shown at the top in the Text To Display box. And your cursor will be shown in the white Address input box at the bottom.

Simply paste the website address you want into that address box and then click OK.

You can also click on the dropdown arrow at the end of that address line to see a list of recent websites to choose from instead of pasting in the address.

One other way to open the Insert Hyperlink dialogue box is using Ctrl + K, although this is not something I've ever done often enough to use it.

In Excel 2019 all of this is referred to as inserting links. Previously it was referred to as inserting hyperlinks. I assume this is because of the other linking options you've always had which you can see listed on that left-hand side.

As you can see, there are also options to use an existing file, a place in the current document, a new document, or an email address.

Existing Files

To link to an existing file it's still the default option on the left-hand side. But this time you can navigate to the file you want using the folders and/or files listed in that center section there that starts with Look In.

You have the option to start with Current Folder, Browsed Pages, or Recent Files.

If you click on Browsed Pages or Recent Files it looks a little intimidating and messy but it's just showing you the full file path to each file or website you've recently opened.

Personally, I prefer the Current Folder option and navigating to my file that way because it's the more standard appearance I'm used to. Simply navigate to where the file you want is stored and click on it to place the file path in the address space. Then click OK.

The link in your document will look just like the link for a website did. Your text will be blue and underlined, but if you hold your mouse over the linked text you'll see that the link to follow is a file path as opposed to a website link.

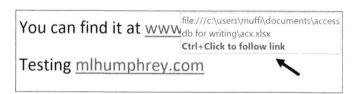

Even though you can link to other files, I rarely do so because I've worked with documents one too many times that do this and the links were often broken by the time the document came to me.

One reason this happens is when someone links to a document that's only available on their computer. It works fine for them, but not for anyone else. (Or they link to a document on an internal server so everyone in their organization can access it, but external users can't.)

Another reason this happens is the linked document is moved or renamed after the link is created.

So be careful with this one. It seems like a great idea, but it rarely is.

Another Section of the Document

You can also link to another section of your document.

This is how Word's table of contents works for example. It uses the Headings-styled entries in your document to create that table and then you can link to each of those entries so that someone clicks on the entry in the table of contents and goes straight to that page.

To link to another section in your document, you need to select the Place In This Document option on the left-hand side of the Insert Hyperlink dialogue box. That will then show you all of the Headings and Bookmarks in your document.

You will not be able to link to another portion of your document (other than the top of the document) unless you've used a headings style or bookmark in your document. (I'll cover bookmarks next.)

In this screenshot, I've already assigned three different heading styles to chapters 1, 2, and 3 and created a bookmark called "Test".

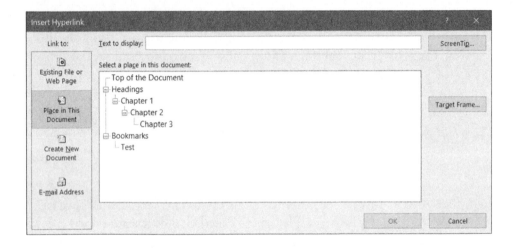

I can now choose any of these locations to link to from my current location.

In this example I didn't pre-selected text to link to when I opened the dialogue box so that field needs to be populated as well. When I click OK Word will insert the text into the document as well as turn it into a link to the section I select.

Unlike website links, by default for the headings-styled links in a document the text just says "Current Document" when you hold your mouse over it.

A bookmark will give the name assigned to the bookmark.

To change the text displayed for a link when someone hold their mouse over it, in the Insert Hyperlink dialogue box, click on ScreenTip in the top right corner to open an additional dialogue box where you can type in the text you want displayed. (Right-clicking on a link and choosing Edit Hyperlink will bring the dialogue box back up if you already closed it.)

Email Address

The final link option you have is an email address.

To link to an email address click the E-mail Address option on the left-hand side of the dialogue box and then enter the text to display, e-mail address, and any subject line you want that e-mail to use.

The good news is that by default the text a user sees when they hover their mouse over the email link shows the email address.

I would recommend that you do not change that, because when someone clicks on an email link like that Word tries to open their mail program. For someone like me who does not have their Outlook activated on their computer, that doesn't work.

But, as long as the link also displays the email address that needs to be used someone can still go to their email account and manually send an email to that address.

Edit a Link

Once you create a link, you can always go back to that link and edit it by right-clicking on the link and choosing Edit Hyperlink from the dropdown menu. This will open the Edit Hyperlink dialogue box which is pretty much identical to the Insert Hyperlink dialogue box.

Remove a Link

You can remove a hyperlink from your document by right-clicking on it and choosing Remove Hyperlink from the dropdown menu.

You can also click on Remove Link from the Edit Hyperlink dialogue box.

Open A Link

To actually use a hyperlink, hold down the control key while clicking on the link. Or, right-click on the link and choose Open Hyperlink from the dropdown menu.

Links to a document may generate a warning message.

Copy a Link

You can also copy a link by right-clicking on the link and choosing Copy Hyperlink from the dropdown menu. When you then paste it in another location that will paste the text associated with the link as well as the link path.

Bookmarks

Bookmarks work much the same way that links do. To insert a bookmark, click on the location in your document where you want to place it, go to the Links section of the Insert tab, and click on Bookmark.

The Bookmark dialogue box will appear. Type in a name for your bookmark and hit Enter.

You should choose a name for your bookmark that will make sense to you when it's in a list since the name of the bookmark is generally all you'll see.

It also has to be one word that starts with a letter. As soon as you use a space in the name, the option to add the bookmark will disappear. You can use an underscore in place of a space, so test_bookmark would work just fine.

Once you've added a bookmark in your document you can click on the Bookmark option again to bring up the Bookmark dialogue box which will let you select any bookmark you've created and go to that bookmark, delete it, or rename it.

Another way to access your bookmarks is to use Ctrl + G to open the Find and Replace dialogue box onto the Go To tab. Click on Bookmark in the Go To What box and then choose the bookmark you want and Word will take you to that location in your document.

Deleting text that included a bookmark will also delete the bookmark.

Go To Option

I'll be honest, I've never used the Go To option in over twenty years of working with Word, but having written about it just above with respect to bookmarks, I figured it was worth a brief mention here.

As noted above, the control shortcut Ctrl + G, will open the Find and Replace dialogue box onto the Go To tab. You then have a number of choices for where to go.

For example, here I've chosen to go to the second section in my document. It turns out to be where the Introduction starts. (The first section in this case is the title page.)

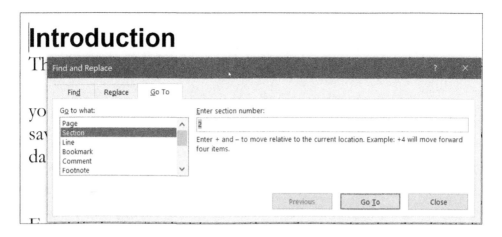

I could picture using this in a long document to check that all of my sections have headers and footers and page numbers that work the way they're supposed to.

Other options in that list are page number, line number, bookmark (as discussed above), comment (where you can specify a specific individual if you want), footnote number, endnote number, any field that was used in the document, any table, any graphic, any equation, any object, and any heading.

Like I said, I've never needed this, but I could see using it to scan a final document for formatting or style issues by walking through each of those items or using it to find something I don't want in the final version like a field.

Change Case

Now let's cover how to change the case of your text.

For example, say you have a bunch of text that's in all caps (LIKE THIS) and you want to convert it to title case (Like This). Or your text is in lower case (like this) and you want to convert it to all caps (LIKE THIS).

You could retype it, but that's annoying and could introduce errors.

You could also right-click and choose Font from the dropdown menu to access the Font dialogue box. But the only choices there are all caps or small caps.

The best way to handle this is to go to the Font section of the Home tab and click on the dropdown arrow next to the Aa in the top row which is for Change Case.

This will give you the option to format your text as sentence case (where the first letter of each new sentence is capitalized), lower case (where no letters are capitalized), upper case (where all letters are capitalized), or to capitalize each word (where, you guessed it, each word is capitalized, something I sometimes refer to as title case).

There's also toggle case which reverses the capitalization of every letter.

Once you apply the change case option to a section of text it will be permanently changed.

Watermarks

Another simple but useful trick to know is how to place watermarks in a document.

Have you ever seen a document that had DRAFT in gray text across the background? That was what's called a watermark. It can be very handy to use when you circulate a document for review but you want to make it clear that the document should not be considered a final version.

I've seen people put DRAFT in their header or footer instead, but that's not as effective in my opinion because it can be easily overlooked or even removed if the document is copied.

Using a watermark is handy because the watermark is visible behind the text, which means no one can copy the document and conveniently leave off the header or footer.

Also, most people know how to edit a header or footer, but a lot of people don't know how to remove a watermark, so it's more likely to stay in place until you're ready to remove it.

Okay, so how to do this:

Go to the Page Background section of the Design tab and click on the arrow under Watermark on the far right-hand side.

Word provides a number of default options. Here you can see options that say Confidential or Do Not Copy. If you scroll down you'll see options that say Draft, Sample, ASAP, and Urgent.

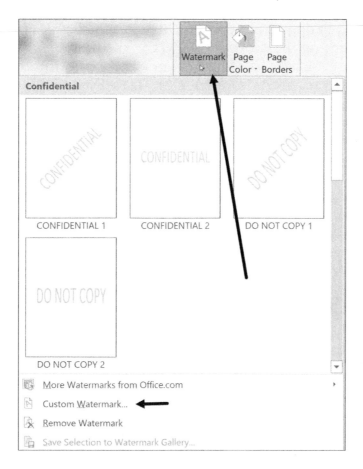

If you need your watermark to say something else, or you want to change the color or font, or insert an image as your watermark instead, you can choose the Custom Watermark option at the bottom of the dropdown.

This brings up the Printed Watermark dialogue box. From there you can click on Picture Watermark or Text Watermark and then add your image or your text. You can also adjust the font, color, etc. to your liking.

When you're done, click Apply.

To make edits to an existing watermark, click on Custom Watermark again.

To remove a watermark, choose Remove Watermark from the dropdown menu.

Line Numbering

The only place I've ever seen line numbering in a document was for interview transcripts or legal briefs, but in case you need it...

To add line numbering to your document, go to the Page Setup section of the Layout tab and click on the dropdown next to Line Numbers.

You can choose to have continuous line numbering throughout the entire document or have it restart on each page or for each section.

To specify what number to start numbering with and/or what increments to use for your numbering (so you could start at 10 and go up by 10 instead of it starting at 1 and going up by one each line), click on Line Numbering Options in the dropdown menu. This will bring up the Page Setup dialogue box. From there click on Line Numbers to bring up the Line Numbers dialogue box.

You can also specify here how far from the text the numbers should be.

To bring up that Page Setup dialogue box other ways you can either click on the expansion arrow for the Page Setup section of the Layout tab or go to the File tab, select Print, and then click on Page Setup at the bottom of the list of options. Once in the Page Setup dialogue box, click on Line Numbers at the bottom of the Layout tab to bring up the Line Numbers dialogue box.

To remove line numbers, use the line numbers dropdown and choose None. Or you can bring up the Line Numbers dialogue box and uncheck the add line numbering option at the top.

Insert A Symbol

There may be times when you need to insert a symbol into your document. For example, I've done so in the past when I needed to use a foreign currency symbol such as the Euro or Pound mark. I've also used it for copyright and trademark symbols as well. (Although Word does have shortcuts for those last two. As mentioned in *Word 2019 Beginner* I turned off the AutoCorrect option for copyright because I'm far more likely to need to write (c) than I am to need that symbol, but if you haven't turned that off then typing a c in parens will automatically create a copyright symbol.)

To insert a symbol into your document, click on the location in your document where you want to insert the symbol. Then go to the Symbols section on the far right-hand side of the Insert tab and click on the Symbol dropdown.

You'll see a selection of about twenty recently used symbols and/or commonly used symbols as well as an option for More Symbols below that.

If you see the symbol you want, click on it and it will be inserted into the document. If you don't see the symbol you want then click on More Symbols which will open the Symbol dialogue box.

Here you can see both the dropdown (on the right-hand side) as well as the Symbol dialogue box (on the left-hand side).

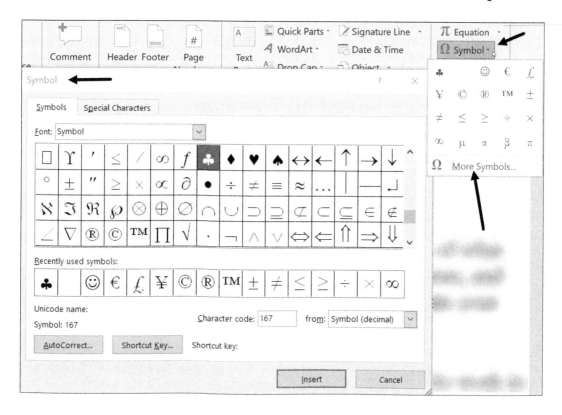

In the Symbol dialogue box, either double-click on a symbol to insert it into the document or click on it once and then click on Insert

If you don't see the symbol you want, you can scroll through the available options using the arrows on the right-hand side until you find the symbol you want.

To shorten that process you can also use the Font dropdown menu to move to a specific type of symbol. For example, if you're looking for shapes like mailboxes or folders or two-dimensional arrows, change the Font to one of the Wingdings options since that's where most images and shapes can be found.

There is also a Special Characters tab that you can click on to find the symbols for items like copyright, registered, and trademarked.

Once a symbol has been inserted into your document, you can select it in the document and change the formatting just like you would normal text to change the color or size, etc.

Just be careful if you try to change the font.

It doesn't matter for every symbol, but for some of the symbols changing the font changes the symbol.

Also note that the dialogue box doesn't close after you insert the symbol which means you can leave it open while you're working if you think you'll need to insert more symbols.

Insert an Equation

You can actually insert a mathematical equation into your document. This one probably won't come up often, but if it does, it's very useful.

The option is located right above the Symbol option in the Symbols section of the Insert tab under the title Equation. Click on that dropdown and you will see a number of pre-formatted equations listed such as the area of a circle and Pythagorean theorem.

You can scroll down on the right-hand side to see more equations.

If the one you want is shown, just click on it to insert the equation into your document.

When you do that, the equation will appear in your document and an Equation Tools Design tab will also appear that contains a large number of mathematical symbols as well as common pre-formatted structures.

The structures are arranged by category. Each one is a dropdown with additional choices underneath that you can use to build a complex formula.

If you want to go straight to this tab, you can simply click on Equation instead of using the dropdown menu and then build the equation you want from scratch using the Design tab.

When you insert a structure, if it needs a value or values it will show a dotted square for each required value like in this example where I have one value divided by another and Word needs me to input both of those values.

Click on the dotted square to add the letter or number or additional component that you want to use for your value. Above I've clicked on the top square and could now type in my letter, number, etc.

When an equation is inserted into your document it will be inserted in its own box like you can see above.

You can click on the right-hand side of that box to pull up a dropdown menu of formatting choices. The professional format includes subscripts and superscripts. The linear format is written with everything on the same line.

Here is an equation formatted as professional. That also includes the dropdown menu options.

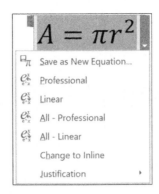

If it were linear that superscript 2 would be replaced with a ^2 where the 2 was the same size as the pi symbol and r.

The All - Professional and All - Linear choices in the dropdown will change *all* formulas in your document to that style.

Justification allows you to change the alignment of your formulas within your document. The default is for your equation to be centered.

If this is something you can use, be sure to play around with it. The overview I've provided here is just the bare minimum.

Specialized Text Formatting

I covered basic formatting of text like bold, italics, and underline in *Word 2019 Beginner*, but I didn't cover some of the less common formatting options, so let's do that now.

Strikethrough

If you ever want to keep text but place a line through the middle of it as if someone has come along and stricken it out, you can use strikethrough.

To do so, select the text, go to the Font section of the Home tab, and choose the strikethrough option. It's the one with the letters abc with a line running through them just to the right of the underline option.

You can also select your text, right-click, choose Font from the dropdown, and then choose Strikethrough from the Effects section of the Font dialogue box. That approach also allows you to choose a double strikethrough option that puts two lines through the text instead of just one.

Subscript Or Superscript

As a refresher, a subscript is when the text is lower than the rest of the text on the line and also generally smaller in appearance. A superscript is when text is higher than the rest of the text on the line and also appears smaller.

The best example of a superscript is the notation for a squared number like we saw above for the equation for the area of a circle which included r^2. Subscripts can come into play when writing chemical compounds like H_2O for water.

If you ever need to do this (for example I have needed superscripts to fix footnotes and endnotes that someone accidentally changed changed to normal-sized text), select the text you want to format and then go to the Font section of the Home tab.

The two options are located just below where you choose the font size and just to the right of the strikethrough option. They're represented by a small bold x with a 2 in the subscript or superscript position, respectively.

(If you hold your mouse over each one, Word will tell you what they are, what they do, and also what control shortcut to use for them.)

You can also access the subscript or superscript options by selecting your text, right-clicking, and choosing Font from the dropdown menu to bring up the Font dialogue box. The subscript and superscript options are in the Effects section of the Font tab.

Place A Box Around Your Text

This is separate from inserting a table into your document which we'll talk about later. If you just want there to be a box around your text (for a resume, for example), you can click anywhere in the paragraph you want a border around, go to the Paragraph section of the Home tab, click on the Borders dropdown, and choose Outside Borders.

That will place a basic border around your paragraph.

If you select more than one paragraph at once the border will go around all of the paragraphs.

The principles for changing the nature of the box in terms of color and style, etc. are the same here as they are for tables so that's where I'll go into that in more detail.

Place a Border Around Your Page

An extension of placing a border around a paragraph is that you can also place a border around your entire page. Do this by going to the Design tab and clicking on Page Borders to bring up the Borders and Shading dialogue box. For a simple border click on Box on the left-hand side under Setting.

You can play around with the options in that dialogue box to get different page border settings other than the default basic black line.

Place a Colored Background Behind Your Text (Shading)

To add shading behind your text, click on the paragraph or select the text you want shaded, go to the Paragraph section of the Home tab, click on the arrow next to the Shading image (the paint bucket pouring paint in the bottom row on the right side), and choose your color from the dropdown menu.

If you just select part of a word or a single word or part of a line it will look much like the Text Highlight Color option in the Font section.

The difference is in how they handle selecting a whole line or more than one line. Highlight will only highlight where there is text. Shading will color the whole line as you can see in this example.

(At the same time, it does not stretch as far as the page border that you can also see as a dotted line in the image above. It limits itself to where text would be.)

Display Text In Multiple Columns

There may be times where you want the text in your document to appear in multiple columns. Think about newspapers, magazines, newsletters, etc. Almost all of those use multiple columns.

To do this you can click anywhere on your text, go to the Page Setup section of the Layout tab, click on the dropdown arrow under Columns, and choose the number of columns you want.

This will apply that number of columns to your entire document. Here I've chosen three columns as an example:

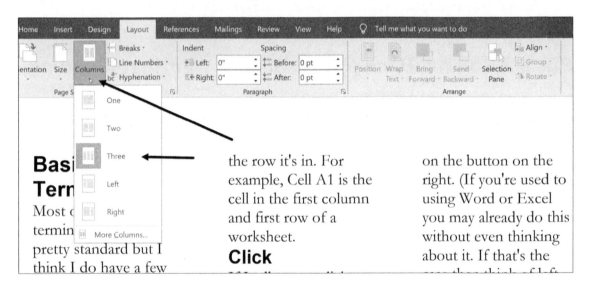

If you only want columns for a subset of your text you can apply them at the paragraph level by selecting just that paragraph or set of paragraphs. This can also be a good time to use Section breaks.

You can see in the screenshot above that your dropdown choices are one, two, or three columns as well as a left column and a right column option. The left and right column options create two columns where either the left or the right column is about half the width of the other column.

If none of those options are what you want, click on More Columns at the bottom of the dropdown menu. This will bring up a Columns dialogue box which allows you to specify the number of columns on the page.

You can also specify the width of each column separately as well as control the amount of space between your columns.

The Line Between option which is located above the preview also allows you to place a physical line between each of the columns.

You can apply the settings to the entire document or just that section.

If you add columns to your document, all of the text will continue down the entire page in the left-most column before moving to the next column on the page and all the way down that column before moving to the next column after that, and so on until all columns have been filled.

As a reminder, if you don't want that—if you want the new column to start with a specific sentence, for example—you can use a column page break to force the text in a column to the next available column.

Add Hyphenation To Your Document

Hyphenation occurs when a word is continued from the current line onto the next line. This is shown by placing a small dash (called a hyphen) at the end of the first part of the word so that the reader knows that the word continues onto the next line.

If you read a lot of books you've probably run across hyphenation and not thought much about it.

It's a good way to have justified text but avoid ugly gaps in a line as Word tries to stretch the text to fit the entire line. This becomes especially important if you like to use big words.

Here's an extreme example of that where I have an incredibly long word. The top example is not using hyphens and you can see that the spacing on that first line is very wide. The second example is using them and you can see how that removes the extra white space between words on that first line because the very lengthy word, supercalifragilisticexpialidocious, is split across lines.

> One of the weirdest words you will ever encounter is supercalifragilisticexpialidocious which I have probably spelled horribly wrong but thankfully spellcheck fixed for me.
>
> One of the weirdest words you will ever encounter is supercalifragilisticexpialidocious which I have probably spelled horribly wrong but thankfully spellcheck fixed for me.

The hyphenation option is located in the Page Setup section of the Layout tab. If you click on Hyphenation you will see a dropdown menu of choices.

In most instances, the Automatic choice will work just fine. The Manual option allows you to click on a specific word and then choose which syllable to hyphenate that word at. It will apply to every use of that word in your document where hyphenation may be needed,

If you want more control over hyphenation then click on Hyphenation options but the only real choices you have there are whether or not to hyphenate words with all caps and how many consecutive hyphens to allow. The default is no limit, but most formatting guides recommend no more than three in a row.

If you choose to automatically hyphenate, it will hyphenate all of your document.

You can exempt a paragraph from hyphenation by right-clicking on the paragraph, choosing Paragraph from the dropdown menu, going to the Line and Page Breaks tab, and clicking on the box next to Don't Hyphenate.

Character Spacing

I tend not to use hyphenation. What I do instead is manually adjust any lines that have a little too much white space in them using the character spacing setting in Word.

To do this, select the paragraph you want to adjust (or the words, you don't have to do the whole paragraph but I usually do), right-click and choose Font from the dropdown menu. From there click over to the Advanced tab and go to the Spacing option.

That option is a dropdown menu that allows you to expand or condense the selected text. I choose condense. Be careful that you don't condense your text too far. I usually won't go above .25 but you'll have to judge things visually because if you're using justified paragraphs it isn't a one-for-one adjustment. You can suddenly have it readjust at .3 or something like that and look better than it did at .1. So you just have to experiment a bit to see what you can do with a particular line.

(Or use hyphenation or a jagged right margin to avoid the issue in the first place.)

Widow/Orphan Control

Another setting you may find yourself wanting to adjust is the widow and orphan control setting. By default Word will have widow and orphan control turned on for your paragraphs.

What this means is that no single line of a paragraph will be left alone either at the bottom of a page or the top of a page. But that can mean that you have two facing pages that don't end at the same point since Word will move that orphaned line to the next page or find a way to keep that widowed line from being alone.

To turn off widow and orphan control, select your text (remember styles, this is probably best done as part of a style), right-click and choose Paragraph from the dropdown menu. This will bring up the Paragraph dialogue box. Go to the Line and Page Breaks tab and uncheck Widow/Orphan control.

(Or if it was turned off and you want it back on, check the box.)

Keep Lines Together

In that same Paragraph dialogue box, you can also manually control a set of lines using the Keep With Next or Keep Lines Together options. This can come in handy at times.

For example, with section headers, I don't want a section header that sits at the bottom of a page by itself without at least one line of the body text to go with it. So part of my style for section headers involves clicking on the Keep With Next option. That ensures that with no effort on my part I'll never have a section header sitting there all by itself at the bottom of a page.

Include a Page Break in the Style

Another option in that Paragraph dialogue box is the Page Break Before option. You can use this one to format a chapter heading style so that Word automatically puts your chapter heading at the top of the next page. It saves the effort of inserting page breaks at every new chapter or section.

(I'm a little too paranoid to use it myself, but it does exist as an option.)

Images

Time to talk about something that's pretty straightforward: How to insert an image into your document.

First, go to the place in your document where you want to insert the image. Next, go to the Illustrations section of the Insert tab and click on Pictures. When you click on Pictures you'll have two choices, This Device and Online Pictures. I'm just going to cover This Device.

When you click on that, Word is going to open into the Pictures folder of your computer by default.

Navigate from there to wherever the picture you want to use is actually stored. For example, my pictures may be in the Pictures folder but are generally stored in sub-folders within that folder.

Once you've found your file, click on it and then click on Insert. The image should now appear in your document at the location you selected.

If you want to move the image to a new location within your document, you can click on it and use Ctrl + X to cut it from its current location followed by Ctrl + V to paste it into the new location.

To make edits to the image, click on it and then use the options that appear in the Picture Tools Format tab.

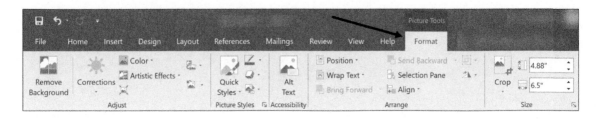

Let's walk through some of those now.

Size

The most common adjustment I make to an image I've inserted into my document is to change its size. As you can see above, size is on the far right-hand side of the Picture Tools Format tab. Here is just that section:

The nice thing in Word is that by default when you change either the width or the height of your image the other value will also adjust to keep the image proportional.

So if I change the 2" above to 3" the 2.67" automatically changes to 4". To do that, I just click into the box with the value I want to change and change it to the value I want. (You can also use the up and down arrows on the right-hand side of each of the boxes, although I never do.).

Another option is to adjust the image within the Word document itself. When you click on your image you will see white circles appear at each of the corners as well as on the sides.

You can left-click on any of those white circles and drag either inward or outward to change the size of the image. If you use the circles in the corners the image will stay proportional in size. If you drag from the sides or from the top or bottom, then just that portion of the image (width or height) will adjust.

Another option is to click on the expansion arrow in the bottom right corner of the Size section. This will bring up the Layout dialogue box on the Size tab. You can uncheck the lock aspect ratio box to adjust the height and width independent of one another. You can also scale the image on a percent basis using this option.

One final way to change the size of an image is in the Format Picture task pane on the right-hand side. If you right-click on the image and choose Format Picture from the bottom of the dropdown menu this will open the task pane.

Click on the last icon, the Picture icon and then the Crop option. This will show you the width and height of the image under Picture Position. You can change either width or height, but the other value will not adjust automatically at the same time.

One more point to make about changing the size of your image.

In general, increasing the size of an existing image will make it more blurry. You need to be working with a high enough quality image to start with to get a large image in a document.

(You'll notice in this document for example, some images are smaller than others. That is directly related to this issue. In order for every image in this document to be "print quality" at 300 dpi or more some can only be so big. Making them bigger than that makes them blurry. And because of how Word scales when you zoom in there is only so much that can be done to get a bigger picture because Word will happily scale text in a document, but does not scale the menus or dialogue boxes. Anyway. Enough random trivia.)

Cropping

If you want to trim off part of an image so that it doesn't display in your document, this is called cropping. I will often do this before I add an image to Word, but you can just as easily crop an image within Word as well.

The first way to crop an image is via the Format Picture task pane. Remember, this can be accessed by right-clicking on your image and choosing Format Picture.

Click on the Picture icon at the end and then click on Crop to bring up the Crop options. The second section there allows you to change the size of the displayed image.

Be careful with this one because if for some reason Word decides that you've imported a rotated image you will have to adjust the width to change the height and the height to change the width.

To Undo, click on the image in the document first. Otherwise it doesn't work.

This is not how I crop an image, however. I covered it first simply because we'd ended with the task pane option for changing image size so were already there.

What I do, is right-click on the image and choose Crop from the mini-formatting menu that appears above the dropdown menu.

This then adds black bars to the sides and corners of the image that I can click and drag to crop my image to the appearance that I want.

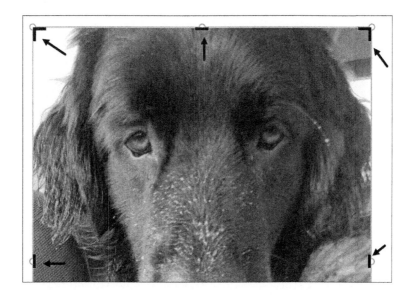

The cropped out portions of the image remain visible but are grayed out (see next page).

Once I'm done cropping the image, I just hit enter or Esc and what remains is only the cropped portion of the image.

I like this method because I can click and move the cropping bars to get exactly the cropped image I want before finalizing it.

There is also a Crop option in the Size section of the Picture Tools Format tab. The first choice in that dropdown, Crop, works just the same.

There are, however, a few other options there as well.

Crop to Shape will let you choose a shape and then will impose the image on the shape. So if I choose the heart option I get a heart that is filled with most of my image.

Just be careful with this one because if Word determines your image is rotated the shape may not insert oriented in the way you expect. With the sample image I've been using here everything was off by 90 degrees and I think that was because of how the image was originally saved outside of Word. So instead of getting an arrow that pointed right, I'd get one that pointed downward and changing the rotation of the image didn't fix that.

So if you run into that issue, fix the orientation of the image outside of Word, reimport it, and try again. (Or with arrows, just choose a different one that's off by 90 degrees from what you really want.)

The next option is Aspect Ratio, which lets you choose to crop your image by set aspect ratios like 1:1, 2:3, 3:2, etc. Click on one of those choices and Word will put a cropped box onto the image that is scaled to that aspect ratio.

For example, this next image shows a box with a 2:3 aspect ratio applied to my image. The gray area is the entire image. The more visible portion in the center is what the cropped image would be if I were to just take the suggested crop as is.

You can click into the visible cropped portion and drag around the *image* behind the cropped box to position the image so that the portion you want is within the cropped space.

You could also at this point break the aspect ratio and click and drag using the black bars instead if you wanted.

The last two options in the Crop dropdown, Fit and Fill, work with Crop to Shape to determine how much of the image will fit into the shape.

Fill fills the entire shape with the picture which means some portions of the image may be lost. Fit makes the entire picture fit into the shape even if that means there is some white space within the shape. You can click and drag the shape once you select either option to get the exact part of the image showing in the shape that you want.

Borders

The next most common adjustment I make to images is to add a border around the edge. Especially if you're dealing with an image that has any whitespace along the edge, adding a border can help to distinguish the image from the background.

The simplest way to add a border to your image is to go to the Picture Styles section of the Picture Tools Format tab and click on the dropdown for Picture Border and then choose a color for your border.

This will insert a plain border around the edge of the image like above where I have a plain black border inserted.

If you want to change the width of the inserted line you can do so using the Weights option at the bottom of the dropdown. There you can choose from a list of line widths ranging in size from ¼ pt up to 6 pt.

(Choosing More Lines from that dropdown will open the Format Picture task pane which will allow you to type in any width you want.)

If you don't want a solid line you can use the Dashes option at the bottom of the dropdown to choose one of seven dashed line options. (More Lines does not seem to give any more choices than those seven.)

If the approximately seventy color choices provided in the dropdown aren't sufficient or you need to use a branded or corporate color, click on More Outline Colors to open the Colors dialogue box which works just the same as it did for font colors or fill colors. (Use the Custom tab to enter RGB or HSL values for your custom color.)

In general, I find that a plain black border is all I really need, but there are many far fancier formatting options available.

Let's walk through those now, starting with the pre-formatted Picture Styles that Word provides.

You can either right-click on your image and then click on the Style option in the mini formatting tab above/below the dropdown menu to see a dropdown menu of these choices.

Or you can click on the image and then go to the Picture Styles section of the Picture Tools Format tab and see the same choices there.

These options involve things like colored frames around the image, bevels, drop shadows, soft edges, rounded corners, different shapes etc.

You can see how each one will look on your image by holding the mouse over the style. It will also give a brief description.

To apply one to your image, just click on it.

If that doesn't give you exactly what you want, there are also a number of additional settings available under Picture Effects in that same section. Each listed setting has a secondary dropdown menu with a variety of options to choose from.

So you can choose various shadow, reflection, glow, soft edges, beveled, and 3-D rotation options. (Just keep your audience in mind, please. Don't let all the fancy bells and whistles get in the way of the information you're trying to impart.)

Another option you have for formatting the border of your picture can be found in the Format Picture task pane.

To access this right-click on the image and choose Format Picture from the dropdown menu. This will bring up the Format Picture task pane on the right-hand side of the workspace. The second option there is effects which is what we just talked about where you can add shadows, reflections, etc.

To change the line around the image you actually need to go to the first option, Fill & Line and then click on the Line section.

Below that you'll see options for the color of the line, the width, the style, etc. which you can change to customize the border around your image.

One final option is to use the Borders option in the Paragraph section of the Home tab. Choose Borders and Shading to bring up the related dialogue box and then choose a Box border from there.

Okay. So lots of choices for that one. Now let's move on to positioning your image relative to your text.

Position and Text Wrapping

I make my life very simple by inserting images on their own line. So as you'll see in this book, there's text, then there's an image, and then there's more text.

But you don't have to do it that way. Especially if you have a small image, you may instead want the image and some of your text on the same line.

This is done one of two ways. The first is through the Position and Wrap Text options in the Arrange section of the Picture Tools Format tab.

You have ten choices for position. All of the position options use the square text wrapping option and basically let you choose to place the image in one of nine segments on that page (top left, top middle, top right, center left, etc.) or to have the image stay inline with the text.

If an image stays inline with the text that means as you add more text above the image it will move down to stay in the same relative position. If you choose one of the other position choices then as you add text it will flow around that image but the image will remain in its section of the page.

If you want to use a different text wrapping option than the default square text option, then you need to choose your text wrapping after you choose your image position.

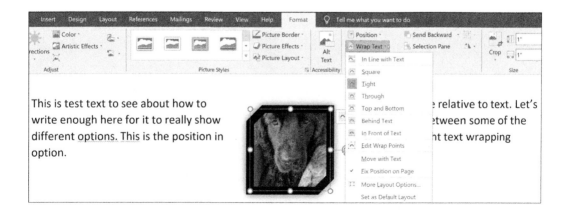

Above I've chosen a center-top position for the image and then a tight text wrap option. Choosing Behind Text would have put the image behind the text and let it carry through the image. Choosing In Front of Text would have placed the image on top of the text and had the text flow behind it. Square, Tight, and Through all look pretty much the same.

One thing to point out here that may not be obvious from the image is that the text flows from left to right across the entire page on each line before continuing to the next line. So it's text, image, text on each line. My instinct on this is that the text should separate into two columns and not flow across like that, which is why I mention it.

The other way to deal with the position or text wrapping of your image is to right-click on it and choose the Size and Position option from the dropdown menu. This brings up the Layout dialogue box. You can then click over to the Position or the Text Wrapping tab and make your selections there.

You can choose to wrap text to the left or the right of the image only and can also specify the exact distance between the text and the image.

Rotate Image

In the same section of the Picture Tools Format tab is one more option I wanted to cover, Rotate. You can click on that option there and choose from a dropdown menu of choices that let you rotate your image 90 degrees right, 90 degrees left, flip it vertical or flip it horizontal.

Choosing More Rotation Options will open the Layout dialogue box to the Size tab where there is an input box where you can enter any rotation value you want or use the up and down arrows to adjust the current value.

Both of those options are great, but they're not how I normally choose to rotate an image. What I do is rotate the image in the document itself. (Usually because when I think of doing so it doesn't occur to me to go to the menu options to do it.)

To do it this way, click on your image in your document and you will see that in addition to the white circles at the corners and on the sides of the image there is an arrow that makes a circle along one side of the image.

To rotate the image, click on that circled arrow and drag in the direction you want to rotate the image. Word seems predisposed to rotate 15 degrees at a time so you can pretty easily rotate 90 degrees without much effort.

Image Adjustments

My general preference is to edit an image in a program outside of Word. But if you don't have access to photo editing software or you just want to make a last-minute edit in Word, there are options for "fixing" or adjusting an image once you've added it to your Word document.

The choices you have can be found in the left-hand side of the Picture Tools Format tab in the Adjust section. Your choices are Remove Background, Corrections, Color, and Artistic Effects. In that same section you can also Compress Pictures, Change Pictures, and Reset Pictures.

I'm going to go through this fast because the average user will not need to know it.

Remove Background

Remove Background lets you take an image and tell Word which parts of the image to keep and which to erase. When you click on that option Word will guess at what to keep (and be very wrong) and then you can either click on Mark Areas to Keep or Mark Areas to Remove and scribble on the image with the green or red marker that Word provides by using a left-click and dragging your cursor around over the image.

When you let up on your left-click, Word will adjust the image to show the new visible portion. I found that sometimes it made interesting choices about what was/was not related in my image and would hide portions I'd already unhid or unhide portions that were on the opposite side of the image from what I was trying to unhide.

If you use this tool, definitely keep an eye on that.

The portion of the image that you remove will be replaced with whatever color or image you have selected as your Fill in the Format Picture task pane section.

Corrections

Corrections contains a number of pre-selected options for correcting your image. There are sharpen/soften options and brightness/contrast options. When you click on the dropdown you will see what they all look like applied to your image and can simply click on one if you want to use it.

The Picture Corrections option at the bottom of the dropdown opens the Format Picture task pane to the Picture section with the Picture Corrections section expanded. This lets you manually adjust your sharpness, brightness, and contrast.

It also lets you reset the image to remove any adjustments you've made.

Color

Color is similar to corrections except the adjustments are all color-related. There are sections for saturation, tone, and recoloring the image. The dropdown will show you the options applied to the image. Just click on one if you want it.

Clicking on Picture Color Options will open the Format Picture task pane where you can manually adjust the temperature and saturation of the image as well as access all of the preset options that were listed in the Picture Tools Format tab.

Artistic Effects

Artistic Effects is again similar to Corrections and Color. There are a number of preset options for manipulating the image and clicking on it will show each of them applied to the image. This includes converting it to a pencil drawing, watercolor, etc. (I'm not terribly in love with any of them, to be honest. Maybe the paint brush is okay. But they are there to use if you need them.)

Clicking on Artistic Effects Options opens the Format Picture task pane to the Effects section and expands the bottommost option, Artistic Effects, but there are no new options shown there. It's the same ones as in the Picture Tools Format tab.

Compress Pictures

This lets you set the resolution of the images in your document. The higher the image resolution the bigger it makes your file, so if you don't need that high a resolution this can be a way to help with that. For book print quality you probably want 300 dpi or more. For computer screens 72 dpi is generally fine. (Their listed values differ slightly from that.)

Of course, this is one that also runs into your Word settings. If you're working with high resolution images you need to adjust your overall Word settings as well or you'll get images compressed when you save the file.

Change Picture

Change Picture lets you change the picture but keep your other settings such as borders or other manipulations. Depending on how much manipulation you've already done this could be a better option than deleting the old image.

Reset Picture

This option lets you remove all of the bells and whistles you've applied to a picture and just go back to the picture as it was when it was originally inserted into the document.

The default option does not return the picture to its original size, but if you click on the dropdown arrow there is an option for Reset Picture and Size.

Image Alignment

One final item to mention is that once you have a number of images in your document and on the same page you can use the Align dropdown menu located in the Arrange section of the Picture Tools Format tab to make sure the images are aligned with one another or along the top, middle, or bottom of the page. I get into that a lot more with the PowerPoint guide where it's much more relevant to the average user. Here I'm just going to let you know it exists if you need it.

As you can see, I have a preference for centering my images. I usually put them Inline with Text and then just use Ctrl + E to center them. If you do that know that the text style you have applied to that line may impact the image. Be sure if you want a centered image to not have a text style applied to the line that includes an indent. Word will indent the image first and then center it so it will be off by half the amount of the indent.

* * *

Okay, then. That was inserting images. Now for how to insert a table of contents into your document.

Table of Contents

For business reports I've often needed a table of contents. And while it may be tempting to just build one yourself, you don't have to and it's probably a better idea to have Word do it for you.

If you have Word build it, you can then refresh the table of contents when you're done editing your document and all section names and page numbers will automatically update. (Much better than having to manually check that each page number is correct, something I've had to do in the past.)

In order to have Word generate a table of contents for you, you need to apply the Heading 1, Heading 2, etc. styles to your section headers and any sub-section headers that you want included in the table of contents. If you've done that, then inserting a table of contents is relatively easy.

I generally only use Heading 1 and Heading 2 in my table of contents, but if you do need more levels than that, you can use those as well.

(Once you apply the Heading 1 and Heading 2 styles to text in your document, Word will automatically add the style for Heading 3 to your styles menu options. And after you apply Heading 3 it will add Heading 4 and so on and so on.)

Assuming you've already applied your styles to the headers in your document, to insert a table of contents go to the place in the document where you want your table of contents. Then go to the References tab and on the left-hand side click on the arrow under Table of Contents in the Table of Contents section.

You can either choose from one of the three provided options or you can choose to create a custom table of contents.

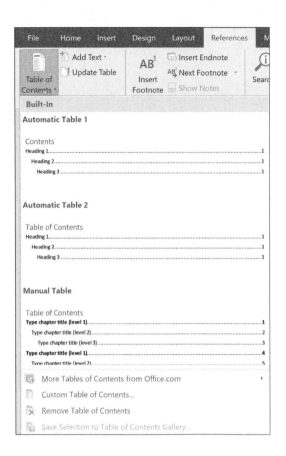

The first two choices use the headings styles as I just discussed. The difference between the two options is whether your table of contents is labeled Contents or Table of Contents.

The third option allows for manual entry. I would not recommend using that third one. Easier if you're going to build it yourself to just build it yourself.

You have the most control using the Custom Table of Contents option at the bottom. Clicking on that option brings up the Table of Contents dialogue box where you can choose how many heading levels to display in the table, whether or not to show page numbers, how to align the page numbers, whether to use a dotted line to connect each entry to its page number, and whether to use hyperlinks in web versions of your document.

Here is an example of a standard table of contents with the table of contents in the background and the Table of Contents dialogue box visible in the foreground. This table used three heading levels.

You can see the default choices for the style in the dialogue box.

If you already have a table of contents in your document and try to insert a custom table of contents, when you click on OK Word will ask if you want to replace your existing table of contents. At that point you can say yes and it will overwrite the existing table of contents with your custom preferences.

For example, here I've chosen to remove the dotted line for the tab leader option and to just display two levels of headings in my table of contents.

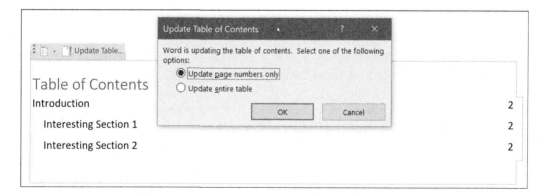

I've also clicked on Update Table above the table of contents to bring up the Update Table of Contents dialogue box which is visible in the foreground.

This dialogue box is important because it lets you update your table of contents values after you make edits in your main document.

There are two choices, Update Page Numbers Only or Update Entire Table. Unless you've for some reason edited the text in your table (as opposed to in the document), I recommend using the Entire Table option. This will capture any changes to the text you're using for your headers as well as any changes in page number due to added or deleted text.

If you notice a typo in one of the lines in your table of contents, fix it in the main document, not in the table of contents. That ensures that both the table of contents and the header in your document reflect the correct text. Updating the entry in the table of contents will only change it in the table of contents.

(Not to mention, if anyone uses Update Entire Table after you make that edit, any changes you made will be overwritten.)

The default font for the table of contents is Calibri, but you can edit that using the Font section of the Home tab. You can also use the paragraph settings to adjust the space between lines.

One more thing: If you hadn't applied the Heading 1, Heading 2, etc. styles to the sections you wanted to include in your table of contents, you can still do that *after* you've created your table of contents.

First, find and select the header you want included in your table of contents. Next, go to the Table of Contents section of the Reference tab and click on Add Text. Then choose which level of the table of contents you want the text added to.

The heading style will then be applied to that text but you'll need to update the table of contents to bring it into the table of contents itself.

(If you use this approach, you're only going to be able to choose a heading level that corresponds to the ones you've included in your table of contents. So if you said two levels that's all you'll be able to choose from under Add Text. If you said four levels, you'll have four choices.)

To remove a table of contents, you can either go back to the Reference tab and choose Remove Table of Contents from the Table of Contents dropdown. Or you can click on the image at the top left of the table next to where it says Update Table. This brings up another table of contents dropdown menu that has a Remove Table of Contents option at the bottom.

Tables

Now on to tables which are incredibly useful for presenting a summary of information. I used these all the time in my corporate career. (Not so much in English class.)

A table is essentially a grid of spaces composed of x number of columns and y number of rows. Once you create that grid any text you enter into one of the spaces is contained within that space.

I find tables are the easiest way to control exactly where text that isn't in simple paragraphs appears on the page.

They also are the easiest way to use formatting with that type of text. For example, the first row of almost any table I've ever used I've shaded it a different color from the rest of the rows in my table. I could do that outside of a table, but it works better with a table.

Inserting

So let's dive in, starting with how to insert a basic table into your document.

You do so by going to the Tables section of the Insert tab and clicking on the dropdown arrow under Table.

There you will see a grid of squares under the heading Insert Table as well as options below that for Insert Table, Draw Table, Excel Spreadsheet, and Quick Tables.

If you had text in your document that you selected before clicking on the dropdown, you'd also see an option for Convert Text to Table.

Let's start with the Insert Table set of squares at the top of the dropdown menu.

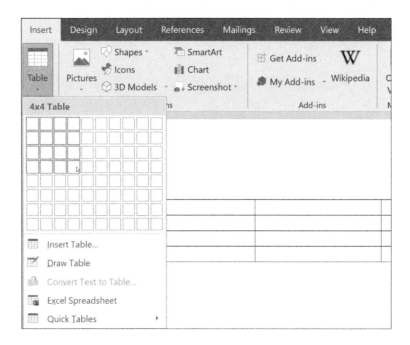

To insert a table using this option, simply hold your mouse over the square that would be in the bottom right corner of the table you want to start with. So above I've put my cursor over the fourth square from the right and fourth square from the top to create a 4x4 table.

As you move your mouse around over the squares you'll see that a table appears within your document with that number of rows and columns.

The title "Insert Table" in the dropdown also changes to reflect the dimensions of the table you're about to insert. Which is why in the image above it says 4x4 Table above the selected squares in the dropdown..

By default, all columns are of an equal width to cover the width of the page or the width of the space you're working in if that happens to be smaller. (For example, you can create a table and then insert another table within a space of that table and the columns in your second table will have a width determined by the size of that space not the whole page.)

Rows are of a standard height that's driven by the current font size in your document.

Unless you're pasting in data, the number of rows is probably not that important. But do try to get the right number of columns initially because they're harder to add later. (The number of columns can be adjusted it's just not quite as easily as adjusting the number of rows.)

To actually insert your table, click on the square.

Your next option for inserting a table is to use the Insert Table option below those squares. When you click on that it will open the Insert Table dialogue box where you can type in the number of rows and columns that you want in your table. Just click into each box and type the number you need, or use the arrows on the sides to increase or decrease the number for rows and columns.

In the AutoFit Behavior section below that, if you use the arrows next to Auto for the Fixed Column Width value you can specify an exact width to use for each column rather than letting the columns fill the page or space you're working in.

Click OK or hit enter when you're done and Word will insert the table into your document.

The Draw Table option is one I don't use. It lets you click on your document and drag to draw a large square that is the overall size of your table and then you can click and drag again to draw the lines for columns and rows. This is probably the best option for a table where the number of columns or the number of rows are not going to stay consistent, like in this table here:

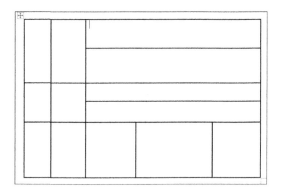

You can get the same effect using split or merge cells, but this was a much quicker and easier option. I just generally don't need a table like the one above.

The final option in the dropdown is Quick Tables. If you scroll past the calendar options there are some basic formatted tables you can use:

They insert exactly as you see them, text and all, so if you use one you'll need to overwrite that text with your own values. (Personally, I'd rather format a new table myself, but if any of those options have a base-level appearance you like it could be a time saver to use one.)

The Excel spreadsheet option will embed an Excel spreadsheet in your document. It initially opens as an Excel rectangle within the document where you can enter values. Once you are done doing so, hit Esc, and it will appear as a basic table in your document. Double-clicking on that table will then open it as an Excel file that can be edited. (Although on my computer it froze and wouldn't open.)

I have used this option in PowerPoint in the past, but I find it to be generally finicky so I tend to avoid it when I can. (You can just as easily create your table and then copy and paste in your data from Excel. Granted, that means the two files aren't connected, but hopefully your Word document is just a summary document anyway.)

Okay, so those are the ways to insert tables. Now let's talk about how to add information and change the structure of your table after the fact.

Contents

Adding Content

To add contents to a table, you can simply click into the table and start typing. Use the Tab key to move to the next cell to the right. If you're at the end of the row it will move you to the first cell in the next row. If you're at the end of the table, Tab from the last cell will create a new row that is added to the end of the table.

Shift + Tab will move one cell to the left. If you're at the beginning of a row it will move up a row to the last cell in the prior row.

Enter creates a line break within a cell. It will not move you down to the next cell in your table. You can, however, use the up and down arrows to move up or down a row in your table and the right and left arrows to move to the next cell to the right or left in a table.

If you enter text that takes up more space than is currently available in that row, the height of the row will increase to keep all of your text visible.

Word 2019 also may by default expand the width of your columns to accommodate the text you enter into a column so that the text all stays on one line. (Once you change this setting it appears to stay changed, however.)

If you want to adjust this setting, you can right-click on the table and choose Table Properties from the dropdown menu to open the Table Properties dialogue box. Next, go to the Table tab and click on Options. From there either check or uncheck "Automatically Resize to Fit Contents".

Your other option is to click on the table and go to the Table Tools Layout tab which should appear as a menu tab.

Click on the dropdown for AutoFit in the Cell Size section and choose Fixed Column Width or AutoFit Contents from the dropdown.

If the information you want to put into your table already exists elsewhere, for example, an Excel spreadsheet, you can copy it from the other location and paste it (Ctrl + V) into your Word document.

To do so, you need to select in your table the same number of rows and columns that exist in your source document. So if you're pasting a 5 cell by 2 cell set of data from Excel, you should select five columns and two rows in your table before you paste.

If you don't do this and instead click into a cell in your table and paste, all of the data will paste into just that one cell.

If you don't select a big enough area to paste into then only the data that matches the area you did select will paste.

Select too many cells and the data will start repeating itself to fill the selected number of cells.

Deleting Content

To delete the contents of a table, you can select all of the cells in the table and then use the Delete key. The table will remain, but all of the text will be removed. If the table is set to AutoFit, when you do this the width of the table may shrink considerably since each column will be only one character wide at that point.

You can also delete the contents in a single cell by clicking into that cell and using the delete or backspace keys. Delete if you're on the left-hand side of what you want to remove, backspace is you're on the right-hand side.

Using the backspace key after selecting the entire table will delete the table as well as its contents.

Using the backspace key with a subset of cells in the table will delete those cells from the table. (More on that in the next section where we talk about how deleting cells works in a table.)

Structure

Once you've inserted a table into your document and started putting some text in the cells, chances are you'll want to adjust the format of your table. Maybe you want to widen a column or a row or add one or delete one.

There are many, many options for doing so. Let's walk through some of them.

Column Width

There are a number of ways to adjust the width of a column in a table.

First, you can place your cursor over the line between two columns. Your cursor should turn into something that looks like two parallel lines with arrows pointing to the left and the right. (You'll probably only be able to see the arrows since the parallel lines will be lined up with the line separating the two columns.)

Once your cursor looks like this, you can left-click on the line between the two columns and drag the line to the left or the right to change the width of the column. This will change the width of both columns at once. The total space taken up by both columns remains fixed.

You can also click and drag the line at either end of the table. (In other words, the left-hand side of the first column or the right-hand side of the last column.) In that case, only the width of that first or last column will change, but the overall width of the table will also change.

The second option is to right-click into a cell in the column you want to change and choose Table Properties from the dropdown menu. This will bring up the Table Properties dialogue box. From there go to the Column tab and change your preferred width by entering an exact width in inches.

You can also change the dropdown there from inches to percent and then enter a number between 1 and 100 that represents the percent of the table width that column should take up. So, for example, 50 would make that column 50 percent of the total table width.

If there's already text in the table this may behave a little strangely because it's not going to hide existing text. You can't have a column that is 99 percent of the table width if the other columns have enough text to take up more than 1 percent of the width of the table.

Also, it will never actually set any column to be 100 percent even if you tell it to if there are other columns in the table.

You can change the width of all columns at once to be the same width using this approach by selecting the whole table or an entire row in the table first and then adjusting the value for column width in the dialogue box.

An easy way to select the whole table is by clicking on the box with four arrows in the top left corner of the table. It should appear as soon as you put your mouse over the table.

Your third option is to click into the table so that the Table Tools Layout tab appears in the menu section up top and then go to the Cell Size section and change the value there for column width. (It's the second one.)

To return to having equally-sized columns you can click on the Distribute Columns option to the right of that input box.

Finally, if you have text that you've entered into a cell, you can have Word AutoFit the width of the cell to the text you've entered by going to the Table Tools Layout tab and clicking on the dropdown arrow under AutoFit in the Cell Size section. From there choose AutoFit Contents.

(Be careful if you do this and only have text in one cell, because all of your other columns will also be adjusted, but to the smallest possible width of just one character wide.)

Row Height

Your options for adjusting the height of a row in your table are mostly the same as for changing the column width, although there will be some row heights you can't achieve because Word forces a minimum row height based upon font size.

First, you can place your cursor over the line dividing any rows in the table and left-click and drag to your desired height. With rows adjusting the height of a row this way WILL NOT adjust the height of any other row.

This does mean that if you adjust the height on any row in the table it will also change the overall height of the table.

Second, you can right-click on any cell in a row and choose Table Properties to bring up the Table Properties dialogue box. From there go to the Row tab and input your desired row height. Your choices are at least or exactly for the value you enter.

(Here is also where you can choose whether or not to let a row break across a page. If you allow this, part of the cell may be on one page and the remainder on another. For rows with a lot of text in them, this may be a necessity.)

Third, you can use the Table Tools Layout tab to specify the row height by changing the number for Height in the Cell Size section. If you want to keep the height of your table as is but make all of your rows the same height, you can click on Distribute Rows.

(AutoFit is not an option for row height. It only works on column width.)

Whichever method you use, be sure to look at the table after you're done, because if you tried to specify a row height that was smaller than Word allows for that font size, it won't have changed.

Table Width

Another attribute of tables that I often change is the overall width of the table.

To do this, right-click on the table and select Table Properties. When the Table Properties dialogue box comes up, go to the Table tab and click on the box for Preferred Width under Size and then specify the width you want for the table in inches.

You can also specify here that your table be X percent of the width of the active area of your document.

Another option is to go to the right-hand side of the table, hover your mouse over that outside column line until you see the two parallel lines with arrows on either side, and then left-click and drag until you have the table width you want.

The problem with this option is that you're basically changing the table size by resizing the last column so it has its limits. If you want to shrink a table, you can only go as far as the minimum width of that last column and then you have to readjust all of the column widths.

Another option if you want the table to be the width of the page is to use AutoFit. Click on the table, go to the Cell Size section of the Table Tools Layout tab, click on the dropdown arrow under AutoFit, and choose AutoFit Window.

Insert a Cell, Row, or Column

If you need to add a cell, row, or column to your table there are a number of ways to do so. We're going to talk about them together because they overlap a great deal.

To insert a cell, click into an existing cell in the table that is where you want to insert the cell. Right-click and on the dropdown menu hold your mouse over the Insert option and then choose Insert Cells from the bottom of new dropdown menu that should appear.

This will open the Insert Cells dialogue box. Your choices are to shift cells right, shift cells down, insert entire row, or insert entire column.

When I choose to shift cells down, Word inserts an entire new row, so that's not an actual option. (But it does make sense that it works that way so that you don't end up with a table with an uneven number of cells in any given row.) So the only real option there for inserting a single cell is to shift cells right.

Now, if you selected a single cell in a single row and inserted a cell doing so would create a table with one cell by itself in its own column at the far end of that row, which is not something I've ever wanted. Generally when working with tables I want to insert an entire row or an entire column.

As you can see with the Insert Cells dialogue box above, those are both also available choices. But you don't actually have to go that far, because (as you can see in the image above that) the Insert dropdown menu also has options for inserting rows and columns.

So you can right-click on your cell, go to Insert, and then choose from the secondary dropdown menu to insert a column to the left or the right of the cell you're clicked into or a row above or below that cell. (The Insert Cells dialogue box option defaults to inserting a row above and a column to the left.)

It is possible to insert more than one cell, row, or column at a time.

If you have a table with five columns in it and want five more columns, the easiest way to do that is to select all five columns and then choose to insert columns to the left or right. Word will insert as many additional columns as you have selected.

Same with rows. Select cells in three rows and choose to insert rows and you'll get three more rows. (And cells, too. Select five cells, you insert five more.)

If you just need a row inserted at the bottom of your table, the easiest way is to use the tab key from the last cell in the table.

(That's why I don't worry so much if I'm building a table where I'm going to input the information manually how many rows there are, because I know that as I reach the last row of the table I can just keep going using the tab key and Word will add the rows for me as I need them.)

Another option you have for inserting rows or columns is located in the Table Tools Layout tab.

Click into the cell in your table where you want to insert and then go to the Rows & Columns section where you have four choices, Insert Above, Insert Below, Insert Left, and Insert Right.

If you hold your mouse over each option it will actually spell out for you that the first two options are for inserting rows and the second two are for columns.

You can click on any of those options to insert a row or column as the case may be. Clicking on the expansion arrow for that section brings up the Insert Cells dialogue box.

(Just a quick note here. If you have your version of Word minimized you may not see the options side-by-side like they are in the image above. When I shrink Word to take up less of my screen the Insert Above option stays where it is but the other three options are listed in one column stacked on top of each other. Just something to be aware of if your display doesn't look quite like mine at any point. The menu adjusts dynamically based on the amount of available space.)

Delete a Cell, Row, or Column

To delete a cell, click on it, right-click, and choose Delete Cells from the dropdown menu. This will bring up the Delete Cells dialogue box where your choices are Shift Cells Left, Shift Cells Up, Delete Entire Row, or Delete Entire Column.

Shift Cells Left will delete the cell as well as its contents. All of the cells in that row to the right of the deleted cell will shift over to fill the empty space. They will keep their contents as well as their original width. The final column of the table will no longer have a cell in it for that row.

(It's not something I'd recommend doing. This works in Excel, but really doesn't in Word.)

Shift Cells Up will delete the content of the cell and will also move the contents of all of the cells in that column that are below that cell up one row,. The number of cells in the table will remain the same, so the cell itself is not actually deleted.

Again, not something I'd necessarily recommend doing, although I have often deleted an entire row or column, so let's cover that now.

To delete a row, you can right-click on any cell in that row and choose Delete Cells and then choose the Delete Entire Row option from the Delete Cells dialogue box.

You can also select at least two of the cells in that row and then use the Backspace key. This will also bring up the Delete Cells dialogue box and allow you to choose Delete Entire Row.

To delete a column works much the same.

You can right-click on a cell in the column you want to delete and choose Delete Cells and then Delete Entire Column from the Delete Cells dialogue box.

Or you can select at least two of the cells in the column you want to delete and use the Backspace key which will bring up the Delete Cells dialogue box where you can select Delete Entire Column.

If you select all of the cells in a column and use the backspace key Word will automatically delete the column without ever bringing up the Delete Cells dialogue box.

If you select all of the cells in a row and then use the Delete Cells dialogue box to Delete Entire Column, that will delete your entire table.

Your final option for deleting cells, columns, and rows is to go to the Table Tools Layout tab, click on the arrow under Delete in the Rows & Columns section and choose Delete Cells, Delete Columns, or Delete Rows from the dropdown. Both Delete Columns and Delete Rows will immediately delete the column(s) or row(s) you have selected. Delete Cells will bring up the Delete Cells dialogue box.

Delete an Entire Table

That Delete dropdown in the Table Tools Layout tab also has a delete table option. But usually what I do is select the whole table by clicking in the top left corner on the box with arrows in it and then Backspace.

You can also select the whole table, right-click, and choose Delete Table from the dropdown menu.

As mentioned above, selecting a table and using Delete will remove the contents of a table but keep the table within your document.

Split or Merge Cells

Above we discussed the Draw Table option for building a table and I mentioned that it was probably the best way to create a table where you want a different number of cells in one row compared to others but that there were other ways to create that same effect by splitting and merging cells.

Splitting a cell lets you take a single cell (or more if you select more) and split it into multiple cells. Merging cells lets you take more than one cell and merge them together to form a single cell.

So, for example, I might have a header I put on a table that uses the first row of that table and merges all of the cells in that row into one single cell.

Like this:

Summary of Quarterly Performance		
Quarter	Good/Bad/Ugly	Comments
Q1	Good	Nice start to the year
Q2	Ugly	That didn't go well

In my opinion, merging the cells in the top row is the easier way to build this table, but I could have also started with a table with one column and split the cells below the first row.

So how do you do this?

To merge cells, select the cells you want to merge, right-click and choose Merge Cells from the dropdown menu.

You can merge across rows and/or columns, so you can merge a set of cells that span two columns and three cells for example.

Unlike in Excel, the text of the cells you merge will remain within your new cell. (In Excel when you do this only the text in the top leftmost cell is kept. In Word all of the text is kept, each cell entry on its own line.)

Another way to merge cells is to select your cells and then go to the Table Tools Layout tab and choose Merge Cells from the Merge section.

Splitting cells works a little differently. You can split a single cell by clicking into it, right-clicking, and choosing Split Cells from the dropdown menu. But that option is only available when you select a single cell in your table. You can't use it if you want to split four cells at once.

If your goal is to split multiple cells (like in the table above if I decided I wanted another column next to Good/Bad/Ugly but wanted to keep everything else sized the way it is), then you need to use the Split Cells option in the Merge section of the Table Tools Layout tab. Select the cells you want to split and then click on Split Cells.

Either approach brings up the Split Cells dialogue box which lets you decide how many rows and columns to split your selection into.

In the example I just mentioned where I want a new set of cells next to the Good/Bad/Ugly column, I would select the cells in that column starting with the header row and then in the Split Cells dialogue box specify the number of rows and columns I want.

The dialogue box will by default show the number of rows in your selection and twice the number of columns, so in this case there would be nothing to change with respect to those values.

However, since my existing cells have text in them, I would need to uncheck the Merge Cells Before Split option before I chose OK.

If you let Word merge the cells before it splits them all of the cell contents will end up split across the cells in your topmost row.

That's how to split cells. They remain part of the same original table, there are just more of them when you're done.

Split a Table

You also have the option to split a table, but when you split a table this creates two separate tables.

I've used this sometimes when manually creating a table of contents in Word that covered more than one page, because it was the easiest way for me to position the table on the second page where I wanted it.

(I know, manual table of contents...Sometimes I don't follow my own best practices. Or am too lazy to add headers throughout a document to enable an automated table of contents.)

So. To split a table, select a cell in the row that you want to be the first row in the second table, go to the Table Tools Layout tab, and click on Split Table in the Merge section.

Word will insert a blank line above that row and you will now have two separate and distinct tables in your document Any adjustments you make to one table, like changing a column width, will not be reflected in the other table.

Repeat A Row At The Top Of Each Page

If you have a table that stretches across multiple pages, chances are you will want to repeat the header row at the top of each page so people know what they're seeing.

Do not do this manually because one little edit and your whole document will be messed up. (Or if you have to change the header row later, you'll need to do so on every, single, page. Ugh. That's a lot of wasted time.)

To tell Word to repeat a row or rows at the top of each page, select at least one cell of each of the rows you want to repeat, go to the Data section of the Table Tools Layout tab, and click on Repeat Header Rows.

The rows you choose to repeat have to be at the top of your table. You can repeat multiple rows, but you can't choose to repeat the second row if you aren't also going to repeat the first row. (The option won't be available.)

Another way to specify that a row needs to repeat on each page is to click into a cell in the row you want to repeat, right-click, choose Table Properties, go to the Row tab of the Table Properties dialogue box, and click on Repeat As Header Row At The Top Of Each Page.

You can do this for multiple rows at once, by selecting one cell from each row before you right-click.

To turn off repeating rows, select a cells in that row(s), go back to the same option and click on it again.

If you have multiple repeating rows, the Table Properties dialogue box will only let you turn them all off at once. The Table Tools Layout tab will let you turn them off individually but it still enforces the rule that you can't repeat the second row if you aren't also repeating the first row and can't repeat the third if you aren't repeating the first and second, etc.

Move a Table

If you have a table that isn't the entire width of the page, chances are you'll need to move it to where you want it on that line. To do this, place your cursor over the table. You should now see a square box appear at the top left corner of the table. It will have arrows pointing in all four cardinal directions.

Left-click on that box and drag the table to where you want it. (This also works for dragging the table to another location in the document.)

If you want to move the table to a different document or a significantly different location in your current document, you can also click on that box in the top left corner, and then Copy (Ctrl + C) or Cut (Ctrl + X) the table, go to the new location, and Paste (Ctrl + V). (The dropdown and Home tab options for copy, cut, and paste will also work.).

The alignment options in the Paragraph section of the Home tab will also work on a table. Just select the table and then click on the alignment option you want (right, left, center). I often use Ctrl + E to center a table as well.

Formatting

Alright. That's how to structure your table, but what about the aesthetics of the table?

Up above in the Draw a Table example you saw an example of a basic table with simple black lines which is pretty much how all tables will look at the start. In the Split or Merge Cells section I showed you a slightly fancier option where I had bolded and centered text as well as shaded cells. But there's far more than that that you can do with a table.

Let's walk through those options now.

Table Styles

We'll start with the easiest option, which is Table Styles. These are the pre-formatted options that Word gives you. They can be found in the Table Tools Design tab as you can see below where we have the Table Styles section of the Design tab as well as two tables below that with different styles applied to them.

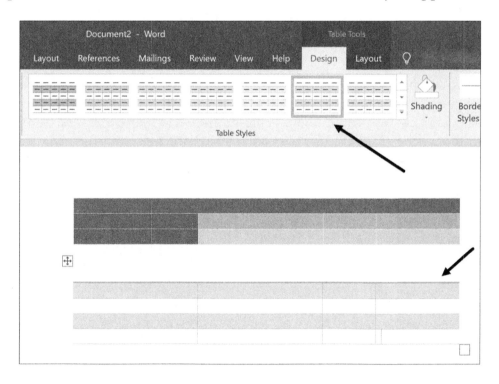

The first style is for a table that has a header row as well as a first column that is also meant to be a label of some sort. The actual rows of data within the table are banded in alternating colors. The second style is much simpler. It just has banded rows but no special formatting for the first row or any of the columns.

You can see what the available styles will look like by clicking on your table and then going to the Table Styles section and holding your cursor over each style. Your table should briefly change to show what the style will look like applied to that table.

To actually apply a style, click on it.

There are more tables than are visible. You can see them by using the up and down arrows to the right-hand side of the visible tables. Clicking on the More arrow just under those options will expand that list of styles to show more at one time and to show their categories: Plain Tables, Grid Tables, and List Tables.

You can then use the scroll bar to see all of the available table styles. I count a total of 105 different Table Style choices.

Clicking on the More option also lets you choose Modify Table Style, Clear, or New Table Style at the bottom.

Be careful of Clear because it erases all lines and special formatting. Your table will still be there so your text will still be separated into cells in that table, but the table itself won't be visible at all. If that's what you want, perfect. Otherwise, avoid this option.

Modify Table Style will open a Modify Style dialogue box where you can change any of the settings on the table style you currently have applied to your table and then overwrite that existing style.

In that dialogue box you can also change the style name and save it as a new style. (If there's a style that's close to what you want this is an easy way to create a style that is exactly what you want, because New Table Style will let you create a brand new style but the base style it's working from is the style with plain black lines and nothing else.)

If you're going to work with table styles begin with the style and then customize from there, because applying a style will often overwrite other formatting.

Table Style Options

In addition to the table styles, there are also six checkboxes to the left of the table styles in a section called Table Style Options. These checkboxes allow you to indicate whether your table should have a header row, total row, banded rows or columns or special formatting for the first column or last column.

From what I can tell they only impact the table appearance when the current table style contains that attribute and you want to remove it. In that case, uncheck the box for the attribute you want to remove from your table.

Shading (Background Fill)

On the right-hand side of the Table Styles section in the Table Tools Design tab is a dropdown for Shading. This is how you fill a cell with background color which is something I often do with header rows in my tables.

To add shading to cells, select the cells where you want to add the shading, go to the Shading dropdown in the Table Tools Design tab, and choose your color. The More Colors option will open the Colors dialogue box which allows you to apply a custom color to your cells using the Custom tab.

Depending on the fill color you choose, you may also need to change the font color in those cells to white so that the text in the cells remains visible.

Another option for adding Shading is to use the Shading option in the Paragraph section of the Home tab. It's also available in the bottom row of the mini formatting menu when you right-click on your table.

There are seventy colors you can choose from in the dropdown and an unlimited number of colors in the Colors dialogue box.

To remove shading, choose the No Color option from the dropdown.

Font, Font Size, Font Color, Etc.

If you want to change the font, font size, text color, add bold or italics to text in a cell, or any other basic text formatting, you can do so in the same way that you would format text in other parts of your document using the Font and Paragraph sections of the Home tab or the mini formatting menu.

For the entire table, click on the box in the top left corner to select all cells in the table first. If it's for specific cells, select those cells. If it's for specific text, select the word(s) you want to format within a cell.

Be careful with changing your font or font size, because the height of the rows in your table will automatically resize to accommodate your text. Depending on your settings, the column widths may change as well.

Table Line Styles, Weight, and Color

Another aspect of a table that you might want to adjust is the appearance of the lines that form the table.

For example, I have manually created a table of contents in the past using a table but didn't want a visible table, so changed the line style to No Border.

I've also had situations where I wanted a thicker outer border around a table and then thinner lines within the table. Also, I've sometimes wanted thicker lines in general (like in the example above for drawing a table where I manually changed each of those lines to a thicker than normal line width to make them more visible.)

To change the lines on a table that you've already created, click on the table and then go to the Borders section of the Table Tools Design tab and choose the line style, weight (thickness), and color you want.

For example, here I've chosen a double border line with a 2 and ¼ pt thickness and a blue color.

At that point, the lines on your table will not have changed. They will remain whatever they were before.

As soon as you make a change to the border style, the Border Painter should turn on. Your cursor will look like a paint brush (If it doesn't, click on Border Painter on the right-hand side of the section.)

To change individual lines to the new line format, simply click on them while the Border Painter is turned on. (Esc will turn it off.)

If you have a large number of lines to change, such as your entire table, use the Borders dropdown menu choices instead which are to the left of the Border Painter option.

In order for this to work, you need to select your entire table first, and then choose your border style. If you just select a cell or click into your table, whatever choice you make will only be applied to that one cell.

For example, if I wanted to apply my new line style to every line in my table, I'd select the entire table and then choose the All Borders option from the Borders dropdown menu.

It is possible to use multiple line styles in the same table, but be careful about the order in which you apply them. Depending on what you're trying to do, sometimes it's easier to apply one style as All Borders and then go back through to make refinements on subsections of the table.

I will often do all borders for a plain black line and then apply a thicker border to just the perimeter of the table.

Another option for applying borders or editing the line style of a table is to click on the Expansion arrow from the corner of the Borders section of the Table Tools Design tab or to choose Borders and Shading from the very bottom of the Borders dropdown menu to open the Borders and Shading dialogue box.

The Borders dropdowns in the Paragraph section of the Home tab and the mini formatting menu also will work although you'll need to open the Borders and Shading dialogue box to change the color, weight, and line style.

Using the Border Sampler

If you have a line in a table that is formatted exactly the way you want already, you can sample it and copy its formatting for use on other lines.

To do this, go to the Borders section of the Table Tools Design tab and click on the arrow under Border Styles and then click on the Border Sampler option at the bottom of the dropdown. (You can also right-click on your table, choose Border Styles and then Border Sample from there.)

Your cursor will turn into a little eye dropper. Click on the line with the formatting you want and you cursor will then turn into the Border Painter paint brush and all of your color, width, and style settings will adjust to match the line you sampled from.

From there you can then apply that formatting using any of the options we discussed above.

Be careful with this one because the first line you click on will be sampled and any line after that will take the formatting of the first line. I messed this up a few times by clicking on one line and then another expecting the second click to take that second line's formatting until I remembered enough to not do that.

If you sample from the wrong line the first time, use Esc to turn the Border Painter off and then try again.

Text Direction

By default, the text in the cells in a table will be aligned just like normal text and will run from left to right across the cell. You can change the text direction, however, so that the text runs up and down.

The best way to see the available options is to right-click on your table and choose Text Direction from the dropdown menu.

This will bring up the Text Direction - Table Cell dialogue box.

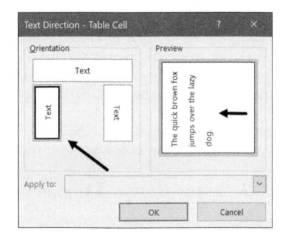

The left-hand side of the dialogue box shows the three available orientation options. The right-hand side shows a preview of the currently-selected option.

To apply a text direction, select the cells in your table, right-click, choose Text Direction, click on the direction you want, and then click on OK.

You can also use the Text Direction option in the Alignment section of the Table Tools Layout tab. Clicking on it will change the direction of the text in your selected cells. Each time you click on it, the text in your table will rotate to the next option. (There is no dropdown so you have to rotate through.)

Text Alignment

In addition to the direction of the text, you can also change the alignment of the text. Alignment works along two dimensions. One of the dimensions is top, center, or bottom. The other dimension is left, center, or right.

Combine the two and you get nine choices. For example, Top Left, Top Center, and Top Right for the three top of a cell alignment choices.

You can left, center, or right-align text in a table using the Paragraph section of the Home tab,. Control shortcuts (Ctrl + E, R, and L) will also work for center, right, and left alignment if you're working with a subset of the cells in a table.

But the only place to also assign top, middle or bottom placement of your text is in the Alignment section of the Table Tools Layout tab. There you can see visual representations of each choice and simply click on the one you want to apply to your selected cells

Here are examples of all nine choices applied to cells in a table:

Top Left	Top Center	Top Right
Center Left	Center	Center Right
Bottom Left	Bottom Center	Bottom Right

Spacing Between Cells

You can also format a table so that there are spaces between each of the cells in the table. To do so, click on your table, go to the Alignment section of the Table Tools Layout tab, and click on Cell Margins

This will bring up the Table Options dialogue box. If you click on Allow Spacing Between Cells and specify a value that will place a space between each cell in your table. If you use a visible border line on the interior of your table each cell will have its own border and then there will be white space between all of the cells.

You can also bring up the Table Options dialogue box by right-clicking on your table, choosing Table Properties from the dropdown menu, and then clicking on Options from the Table tab.

Other

My personal preference is to do all calculations, sorting, and data analysis in Excel and then just copy the results into Word when I'm done. However, Word does allow for some manipulation of your data within a table. (Aside from the embedded Excel file option we discussed earlier that kept crashing on me.)

So I'm going to cover these options here, but this is not how I recommend doing this.

Sorting

You can actually sort lines of text in Word without having them in a table. For example, you could have a list of five words in Word, each on a separate line, and have Word sort them by using the A to Z option in the Paragraph section of the Home tab.

It's far more likely, though, that you'd want to Sort entries in a table.

For example, if I decide to use Word to keep track of all of the books I've read in a year. I'm just going to enter them in my table one-by-one. But come the end of the year I might decide I want that list to be alphabetical by title or author rather than sorted by date.

To sort the entries in a table, select the whole table (by clicking the little square with four arrows in the top left corner), go to the Table Tools Layout tab and click on the Sort option in the Data section on the right-hand side. (It has a big stacked AZ with an arrow.)

This will bring up the Sort dialogue box.

If you have a header row in your table, tell Word and it will label your options using the labels in your header row. Otherwise it will just number the columns.

(The option to say you have a header row is at the bottom of the dialogue box not the top like it is in Excel.)

You can then choose to sort your table by the values in up to three different columns. The first column you list will be the main one used in the sort. The second listed column will only be used if two rows have the same value for the first column. Same for the third, it will only be used if the values in the first AND second column are the same for at least two entries.

For each column you can choose to sort in either ascending or descending order and you can specify to Word whether the contents of the cells should be treated as text, numbers, or dates. (Word will try to make that assignment itself, but you can change it.)

Once you've made your selections click on OK.

Formulas

Word does have a formula option in the Table Tools Layout tab but you'll need to know a bit about formulas in Excel to use it effectively. It also appears to only work on one cell at a time.

To use this option, click into a cell in your table and then go to the Table Tools Layout tab and click on Formula. This will bring up a Formula dialogue box.

Word may suggest a formula to you based on the contents of the table, but it also may not. If it doesn't, you can go down to the Paste function option at the bottom of the dialogue box and choose from the list of functions in the dropdown menu. (The Help text for this option lists out what each function can do.)

Choosing to paste a function will paste an empty version of that function into the Formula line. You'll then need be able to complete it yourself.

The basic use of formulas in Word relies on using the positional arguments, LEFT, RIGHT, ABOVE, and BELOW.

For example,

=SUM(LEFT)

will sum all numbers in the cells in that row that are to the left of the cell you're in.

=AVERAGE(ABOVE)

will average the numbers in the cells in the same column that are above the cell.

=PRODUCT(RIGHT)

will take the product of the values in the cells in that row that are to the right of the current cell.

You can combine two of the positional arguments, so:

=SUM(LEFT,ABOVE)

will sum all cells in that row to the left and all cells in that column that are above the cell with the formula.

After you've placed a formula in your table, select the table and use F9 to update the formula. Otherwise the value in your formula will not reflect the current value. You can also just highlight the value in that one cell and use F9.

Be careful with text values in your cell range. They may not behave as expected in your formula.

If you don't want to use the positional arguments, you can also use A1 notation which is how you reference a cell in Excel. So Cell A1 is in the first column and first row. Cell C3 is in the third column and third row.

To specify the format of your result, use the Number format dropdown choices in the dialogue box.

(Unfortunately, those number formats are only available for when you use a formula, so if you have fixed numeric values that you want formatted in a specific way you need to format those in Excel and then copy them into Word or manually create the appearance of the format you want for each cell.)

Convert to Text

There have been times when I copied information into Word and it copied in as a table but I didn't want it to be a table

The way to fix this is to select the table, go to the Data section of the Table Tools Layout tab, and click on Convert to Text.

A Convert Table to Text dialogue box will appear that lets you choose how to separate each entry. You can choose paragraph marks, tabs, commas, or your own separator. Once done, click OK.

The text will no longer be in a table, but the values from the table will still be in your document.

If you use paragraph marks each entry from the table will appear on its own line. If you use a different separator option, values for each row of the table will appear on a line together with each column's values separated by your chosen separator.

(Sometimes when I do this I need everything listed together in a simple paragraph with each enttry separated by a comma. To get that result I combine Convert to Text with Find and Replace to change the line break for each row to a comma and a space.)

Compare Two Documents

Alright. So that was tables. There's a lot there. Track Changes is up next which is another complex one. So to give us all a breather I thought I'd cover how to compare two documents.

I have needed this multiple times in my career. One of the big ones is when someone goes through a document I've sent them and makes edits but they don't use track changes and I have no idea what has been changed.

With the type of work I've done in the past a single changed comma can be significant, so to make sure I catch and review every single change I will compare the document they sent back to the document I sent them.

What comparing documents does is it creates a new document that takes the first document and notes all changes on it that would have led to the second document. Every deletion, insertion, format change, etc. is marked.

It basically creates a version that looks like track changes was used.

To do this, first, be sure that both documents you want to use have been saved. Word won't compare unsaved documents.

Next, open any document in Word. It can be one of the documents you want to use, but Word will make you find the documents you want to compare anyway, so it doesn't have to be. The key is to have Word open so you can access the Review tab.

Go to the Review tab and click on the dropdown under the Compare section and choose the Compare option. (We're not going to discuss Combine here. My super-attentive-to-detail self refuses to use it. There are just too many ways for a combine option to go wrong for me to trust it.)

When you choose the compare option, you will see the Compare Documents dialogue box.

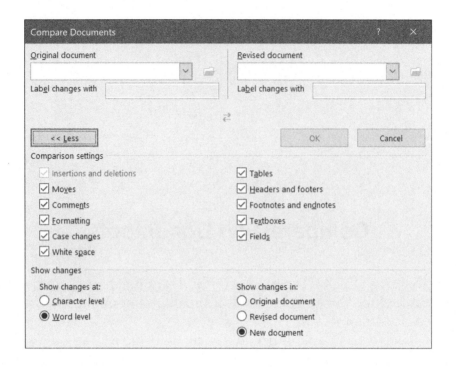

I've clicked on the More button here to show you all of the options available. The default view just shows you the two dropdown menus where you choose which document to treat as the original and which to treat as the new document.

Next to each of the dropdown menus is a small folder image.

You can either see if the documents you need are in the dropdown or you can use the folder image to bring up a dialogue box that lets you navigate to where you have the document saved.

Which document you list as the original and which you list as the revised document matters because Word will mark changes based upon what has been done to the document you identify as the original.

For example, take the following sentence:

"What are you doing here, Carl?"

Let's say the name was wrong and should've been Bob, so the person editing the document changed it. If you compare the documents in the correct order you should see a line through Carl and then Bob as the replacement text. If you compare them in the wrong order, though, it will look like Bob was replaced with Carl.

So always be careful to select the correct original document and correct revised document.

Once you select both documents, Word will list a name under the Revised Document to show who will be listed as the author of any edits. I usually have to change this, because I want the changes labeled with the name of the person who sent me the document, not my name.

In the More section you have additional options to choose what changes are identified.

I never mess with the default settings on compare, they all work fine for me, although there have probably been times I could've turned off tracking formatting changes and been much happier since I visually inspect for formatting issues.

Once you've made all of your choices, click on OK and Word will do the comparison.

If you've left the other settings untouched, this will be done in a new document. You result will look something like this:

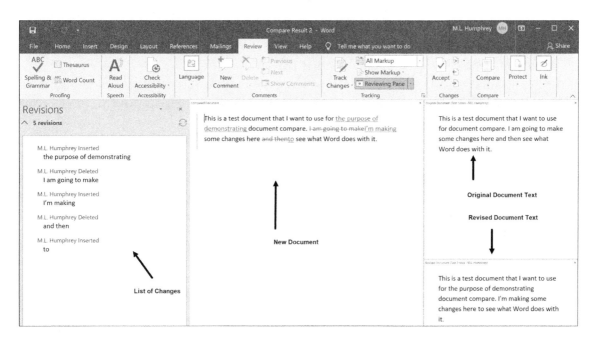

On the left-hand side will be a listing of each change that was made between the two documents.

In the center will be the new document that was created using track changes. Inserted text is red and underlined. Deleted text is read and has a strikethrough. (See the section on track changes for a longer discussion on how this works.)

On the right-hand side the text in both the original and revised documents is shown.

This makes it very easy to walk through and see what the original had, what was changed, and what the revised document looks like.

Keep in mind that sometimes Word labels things as changes that really aren't. For example, I just ran Compare on a paperback I had recently reformatted and it shows font changes that I hadn't technically made to the document. What I had done is accidentally deleted a header or two and had to retype the text. Even though I didn't change the font, Word labeled that as a font change.

Compare also doesn't do well if large chunks of text have been added or moved around.

I've seen it miss that a paragraph of text was inserted from later in the document and then flag everything from that point forward as a change even though it really wasn't.

(If that ever happens to you, I'd recommend creating a middle version of the document where you just move the blocks of text but don't have the edits yet and then running Compare on that interim document. That way you still get to see the smaller changes that were made.)

Basically, it's a useful tool, but it's not perfect.

I should also add that I don't think I've ever had a situation where Compare failed to identify a change. When it errs it errs on the side of identifying more changes than there actually were.

Okay, time to talk about track changes so that you know how to look at the changes Compare flagged between your two documents and so that hopefully you just never need to use it because track changes were used up front.

Track Changes

I love track changes. It is a fantastic tool and I'm not sure how I lived without it before it existed. You can write a document, give it to a group for review, they can make their changes in track changes, and you can easily see what they did. It's wonderful.

But…

I've been putting off writing this part of the book because track changes is also somewhat finicky. And it's changed with different versions of Word.

I know, for example, that copy and paste have pretty much stayed the same for the last twenty years. Not the case with track changes. This is probably one of the tools in Word that they like to mess with the most between releases. So the version of track changes you have in Word 2019 is not the same as in any other version of Word and it is probably the tool most likely to change in the next version of Word.

But the basics remain the same. So let's see what we can cover.

Overview

What is track changes?

It's a way for you to see what changes have been made in a document and by whom they were made and when they were made. (So no telling your boss you were working late editing that document when you weren't. One little look at track changes will show you were actually done by four.)

I have had issues in the past when using track changes with tables or formatting changes because the changes either weren't marked appropriately or the ultimate document didn't look the way it appeared it would when track changes were on. More recent versions of Word probably don't have this issue as much, but it's something to be aware of.

This is why I strongly recommend that when you think your document is final, you accept all changes in your document, and then read that document from first page to last. Do not just accept all changes in a document and be done. You need to do one final review of that document to make sure that everything looks the way it should. You don't want to miss something weird like a double period that is only noticeable when the changes have been accepted.

Some of this you can see with different view options, but still. Save all changes and review a clean copy.

AND, this one is huge, be sure that track changes are turned off in your final document and that you've inspected the document to remove all tracked changes and comments.

I have on occasion as both a consultant and regulator been given a document by a client or someone I was investigating that still included track changes or comments. They were turned off, but they were not removed and all it took was one little click to turn them back on and see the interesting discussion about how to phrase something problematic.

Not good. At best something like that just looks sloppy. At worst it could lose you a law suit.

So track changes are great, but know how to use them and how to finalize a document if you do use them.

Okay.

Getting Started

I never turn on track changes until the first draft of my document has been written. It should be obvious to everyone that the base text was a draft and I don't need the entire document to be underlined in red.

Once I'm ready to review a document that's been provided to me for review or to circulate a document for review by others, that's the time to turn on track changes.

To do so, go to the Tracking section of the Review tab, click on the arrow under Track Changes, and choose Track Changes from the dropdown.

This will turn on track changes in your document but nothing will happen until you then make an edit to the document. Assuming you're in full markup view, text you delete will be shown with a strikethrough and text you add will be underlined. Both will be color-coded based upon who made the edit. Each user is assigned a specific color with the first person who made edits usually assigned red, the second blue, and so on and so on.

If you ever need to turn off track changes, you can simply click on that option again in the Tracking section or right-click on a tracked change in your document and click on Track Changes from the dropdown menu.

Either option will turn off track changes for any *new* edits to the document, but it will not remove already tracked changes. Those need to be accepted or rejected.

Track Changes Notation

Here is a sample of text where I've added and deleted some words:

> This is a sample sentence that I ~~want to edit~~ have edited so that you can see how ~~t~~Track ~~c~~Changes works.

The original text read "This is a sample sentence that I want to edit so that you can see how Track Changes works."

I then changed it to read "This is a sample sentence that I have edited so that you can see how track changes works."

The phrase "want to edit" is struck through because it was deleted. The phrase that replaced it "have edited" is underlined because it was added.

Also, the T and C in Track Changes are struck through because they were deleted and replaced with a lower case t and c which are underlined.

(Sometimes, at least in past versions of track changes, Word will show the whole word as edited, not just the one letter, but that could be more when working with document compare than directly in track changes.)

If you look to the left of the line you'll see a gray mark. This indicates that there is a change in that line or at that point in the document.

It's simple enough to see the changes in the example above, but if the change is a deleted or added comma it can be easy to miss. That little mark off to the side is a quick way to scan a page to find if any changes were made on the page.

Another way to do so is to use the Previous and Next options that are available in the Changes section of the Review tab.

Clicking on either of those options will move through your document one change at a time.

As you move through the document, each change will be highlighted in gray.

While Next and Previous are a great way to not miss a single change in your document, sometimes it can be absurdly annoying to use them because literally every change is treated separately.

In the example above where at a glance I can see that Track Changes was replaced with track changes, using Next on those changes would mean four separate stops, one for the deletion of each of the capital letters and one for the insertion of their lower case replacements.

In those situations, if I'm accepting or rejecting changes as I go (which I tend not to do), I'd highlight both words and accept all four changes at once.

Speaking of accepting or rejecting changes, let's cover that now.

Accept or Reject Changes

Track changes will note all the changes you make in your document while it's turned on. But to finalize your document, you ultimately need to accept or reject every change you've made.

My preferred method of doing this is to read through the entire document and make sure I agree with all of the changes and then accept all changes in the document at once.

To do that, go to the Changes section of the Review tab, click on the arrow under Accept, and choose Accept All Changes or Accept All Changes and Stop Tracking.

Which choice you make really depends on who has control of the document at that point and what could happen from that point forward. My personal preference is to not accept the changes until I'm also ready to stop tracking.

But I've also had situations with a team where someone made a problematic last-minute change and no one else knew about it because track changes had already been turned off.

So...Both options have their uses.

In the same way that you can accept all changes in a document at once you can also reject all changes in a document at once using the Reject dropdown menu. (Why you'd go to all that effort and then reject them, I don't know, but it's an option that exists.)

Where I do use the Reject dropdown is for the other choices, Reject and Move To Next or Reject Change:

You can use the Accept and Move to Next and Reject and Move to Next options to move through every change in your document and accept or reject them as you go.

If you accept a change, Word will turn added text to normal text or delete deleted text. If you reject a change, Word will put deleted text back as normal text and delete any added text.

The reason I generally don't take this approach is two-fold. First, because it makes it look like there was no change made, which is not ideal when working in teams.

Say, for example, I'm on a project with five people and I'm supposed to review that document third. I believe the person reviewing it fourth or fifth has the right to see the original document and the edits made by each reviewer. The only way for that to happen is for me to not accept or reject changes.

(Often this is where Comments, which we'll talk about next, can be useful. One person says X, I disagree and type in an edit and then add a comment off to the side to explain why I've disagreed and made that edit, especially if the edit erased a change.)

I think the key in determining whether to edit over an edit or to accept/reject comes down to the nature of the edit. If it's just deleting an extra period or adding a period at the end of a paragraph, who cares? Accept, Reject, fine. Other changes require more consideration than that.

The second reason I tend not to accept or reject changes as I go is that it many changes are paired changes. I deleted X and replaced it with Y. But when walking through a document and accepting/rejecting changes one at a time those changes are split into two separate changes that need to be reviewed and accepted or rejected individually.

(One way around this is to select an entire word or sentence and choose Accept This Change which should accept all changes in that selection.)

For individual changes, you can also right-click directly on a tracked change in your document to accept or reject that change using the dropdown menu.

Reviewing Changes

In the sample I showed above it isn't immediately obvious who made the change or when they made it but there are ways to see that, so let's walk through those now.

Users and Time

One quick way to see who made a change as well as a description of the change is to hold your mouse over each change. When you do that a little box will appear with the user name, time, type of change, and text changed. Like so:

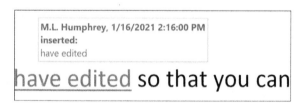

I put my mouse over the text "have edited" and a little comment box appears to show that M.L. Humphrey made that edit on 1/16/2021 at 2:16 PM, that the text was inserted, and that what was inserted was "have edited".

Usually you're not going to do this for every edit. But when you have multiple users on a document it can be a quick way to see which user a color represents. I'll probably hover over each color once to get it into my head which color belongs to which user as I start reviewing the document.

(You need to do this each time, because the color assigned to each user is not fixed. I can be red in one document and blue in the next.)

To easily see who made each edit without holding your mouse over the comment and to also see the full text of any comments, use a reviewing pane.

Reviewing Panes (Revision Pane)

To turn on a reviewing pane, go to the Tracking section of the Review tab and click on Reviewing Pane or the arrow next to it to see the dropdown menu.

By default clicking on Reviewing Pane will open a Revisions pane off to the left side of the main workspace. Using the dropdown menu you can instead choose Reviewing Pane Horizontal to open a Revisions pane below the workspace.

The Revisions pane lists out the user name, type of change, and change for each change made in the document as well as the full text of all comments made in the document. Here is an example of a vertical pane:

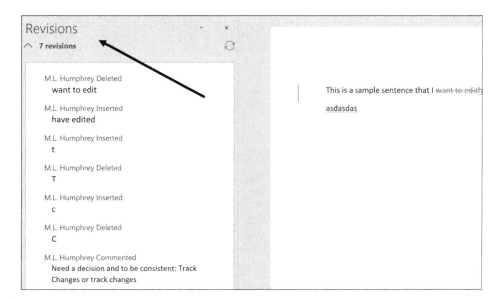

This is another useful way to make sure that you catch each and every change in the document. It's also helpful when working with documents that have extensive comments in them.

It is especially helpful if you have the track change view of your document set to not actually show the changes in the document itself. (A view that I personally DO NOT like, but that seems to be the default these days.)

To close the Reviewing Pane you can click on the option again or click on the X in the top right corner of the pane itself.

Track Changes Views

There are four possible choices for viewing track changes in your document, Simple Markup, All Markup, No Markup, and Original. Each can be accessed through the top dropdown menu on the right side of the Tracking section of the Review tab.

Let's walk through all four.

All Markup

This is a sample sentence that I ~~want to edit~~<u>have edited</u> so that you can see how t~~T~~rack c~~C~~hanges works.

This is the one I prefer because it shows both what's been deleted and what's been added. You can see the strikethrough of the deleted text and the underline of the added text as we discussed previously

Simple Markup

This is a sample sentence that I have edited so that you can see how track changes works.

Simple markup shows the document text in final form but indicates that there was a change made at that point in the document by using a bright red line off to the left side. It also will show any comments that were made.

No Markup

No Markup shows the document text in final form *with no indication that changes have been made in the document.* It also does not show comments.

This in my opinion is the most dangerous view because this is the one where you forget that track changes are actually still turned on, which as I mentioned before can be very problematic under certain circumstances.

This view can have its uses like seeing what the final document will look like with all changes incorporated. But I would highly, highly recommend that you never leave your document in this view. Use it and immediately change it back.

And if you work with someone who uses this view, be sure to always check any document they give you before you send it on as a final document to make sure that track changes have in fact been turned off, all comments have been deleted, and all changes in the document have actually been accepted.

Original

Original shows the document as it was before any changes were made. This can be convenient to toggle on briefly when there are a lot of changes in a section of a document to see what the original text was, but as with No Markup it would be a very bad idea to leave this view on because you would not see that there are tracked changes in the document.

If you then accepted all changes, you'd be accepting changes to the document you didn't realize existed.

I'd recommend before you start reviewing any document that you check the view it is in. (Nothing worse than getting halfway through a document, being furious at someone for not having caught all the issues you are, and then realizing they did catch them but you couldn't see it because the document was in Original view.)

Show Markup Dropdown

You can also choose the type of changes you want to see in your document using the Show Markup dropdown menu in the Tracking section of the Review tab.

In Word 2019 the default is to have Comments, Insertions and Deletions, and Formatting visible, but you can click on any of those options to remove them from your view. (I will often in a complex document turn off formatting.)

If one of those options is already turned off, you can click on it to show that type of change.

The Balloons option works with the full markup view. I generally leave this one as is with comments and formatting changes noted off to the side. That looks like this:

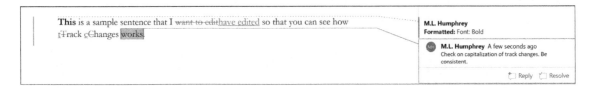

Show Revisions in Balloons shows the final version of the text with insertions still marked but the deletions listed off to the side. Like so:

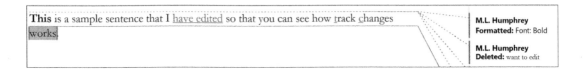

Show All Revisions In Line will not have anything noted off to the side. Formatting only shows if you hold your mouse over the formatted text to see the note. A comment will show as the user's initials in brackets along with the number of the comment [MH1]. You can see the actual comment by holding your mouse over the initials. (Not my preferred view.)

Changes By Multiple Users

As mentioned before, unless something is off about the settings on your document, each individual user who makes changes to the document will be assigned a different color for their changes. When it's just one person making edits to the document using track changes, those changes are generally shown in red. The next user is in blue, etc., etc.

This isn't based on who the user is, so you can be assigned the color red in one document and green in another. If you hold your mouse over any specific change, Word will tell you who the user was who made the changes and when they made them.

(If your document has been stripped of personalization, it's possible to have all changes in the document show up under Author and to not be able to tell who made what change. I would highly recommend that you do not strip personalization from a document that you intend to continue working on.)

If for some reason someone hasn't customized their version of Word (which is rare in corporate settings and probably impossible in newer versions of Word) the changes they make will also show up as Author. If you happen to have two users who have done this, their changes will be combined under the same color and user name and you won't be able to tell them apart.

The dropdown under Show Markup will let you see just the changes made by one user by going to the Specific People option and then unchecking user names. If you have a lot of reviewers for a document, click on All Reviewers to turn off all tracked changes for all users and then go back to click on the user you want to see.

(I don't think I've ever actually reviewed a document one user at a time, but you can. If you ever feel tempted to do so, maybe stop and ask why because that points to a team dynamic issue for me. At the end of the day the whole document has to work together regardless of who made what change. But as I think about this more, maybe if I hired an editor and wanted to see those edits but didn't want to see my own edits in response I could use this? Maybe...I don't know.)

Track Changes With Tables, Lists, and Formatting

I tend to be a little leery about using track changes with tables. I just tried making a bunch of changes to a table in Word and it was okay, but it's still something I approach with care and prefer to do outside of track changes when I can.

For example, I added Shading to cells in my table and as far as I can tell, Word didn't note that as a change. It did capture new text I entered into my table cells. And it flagged an added row to the table in blue and a deleted row in pink. It also caught my bolding of text.

But what it tends to miss is any sort of design work on the table itself. I changed the width of two columns and the height of one row and Word treated all of that as one change that I could either reject or keep.

Also, in this case choosing to reject all changes on my table led to a very strange result. It did not return the table to its original format.

Which is all to say that I would still be wary of using track changes on tables in Word 2019 unless the only changes being made to the table were to the text in the cells in the table.

With lists the issue is looking at them in All Markup mode, because I can't see the indents properly.

If I've done anything to change the numbering, so if I swapped a list from 1, 2, 3 to A, B, C, for example, the way that that's tracked in All Markup can be hard to review.

One solution is to change the Show Markup option to Show Revisions in Balloons instead or while looking at the list to swap over to the No Markup or Simple Markup view.

Honestly, overall I would recommend that any big formatting happen without track changes on and that you try to limit your actions when track changes is turned on to text edits as much as possible. Your life will be simpler if you do it that way.

* * *

Okay. So that was track changes. A very useful tool for group work.

Now to cover something I've always used in connection with track changes, comments, which are actually separate because you can add comments to a document without ever turning on track changes.

Just remember two things before we move on: Always remember to accept/ reject all changes in your document and to turn off track changes when you're done. And never, ever, ever use formatting of your text to replicate the appearance of track changes rather than actually using track changes.

Comments

I often think of comments in conjunction with track changes because that's where they tend to be used the most.

For example, you make an edit in a document and want to say something about it to the others who are reviewing the document so put a comment off to the side. Or have a question about something someone said, so put the question in a comment.

But, actually, comments can be used separate from track changes. You can insert a comment into a document that has never had track changes turned on. And you *definitely* should use the comments function rather than add a comment or question into the text of a document where it doesn't belong. It's far easier to delete comments from a document than track down every bracketed [verify this] hidden in the text of a document.

I have actually seen people do all of the following with a comment added to the text of a document: highlight it, put it in brackets, underline it, bold it, and/or change the color of the text.

The only one of those that is easy to find is the bracketed version.

Maybe the highlight can be found easily without scrolling through every page of the document. But underlined? There might be legitimately underlined text in that document. Bolded? Same.

So do not do that. Do not do any of that.

(I will say this is probably me wasting my breath because when I've seen this happen it was generally by someone very senior who started their career back when there were secretaries whose sole job was to type up these people's handwritten notes. Which means the person who most needs to hear this is not reading this book)

M.L. Humphrey

Okay then. One final point before I move on. There is a time to use brackets in a document. Usually when information is still missing and needs to be filled in before the document can be finalized. Sometimes when I'm writing fiction I don't want to stop and research some minor detail so I'll set that off in brackets. Or you may do this with a class paper. For example, "The first shot fired in the Civil War occurred at [PLACE] on [DATE]."

(Also please, don't ever do what one of my MBA classmates did which was turn in his portion of a paper with [If I'd written this, this is what I would've actually discussed in this paragraph]. Not cool.)

Okay. Sorry about that tangent. Clearly I have had some bad experiences with misused commenting in documents.

Getting back to the point: When you have comments to insert into a Word document it is best to use the Comments feature.

To do so, click on a location in the document where you want your comment linked. (You cannot link a comment to a footnote, so if your comment relates to a footnote, link to either the point in the main text of the document where the footnote occurred or link to a point at the bottom of the page (my preference) that is near the actual text of the footnote.)

Next, go to the Comments section of the Review tab and click on New Comment. Word will usually highlight the nearest word and then link to a comment off to the right side of your text. The comment will have your name on it and you can then type whatever it is you need to say below that.

If you have Original or No Markup selected in the Track Changes section, inserting a comment will open the Revisions pane on the left-hand side of your document. You can type your comment in there just as easily. Click on any comment in that pane to see the word that it links to in the document.

When you're done entering your comment, click back into your document. (Enter will not work since that just adds a line break within the comment itself.)

If your comments are visible on the right-hand side of your document (so you're in Simple Markup or All Markup view), you can reply to an existing comment by clicking on the Reply option which will be visible when you hold your mouse over that comment.

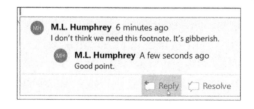

Doing so will create a new sub-comment under the first comment that is labeled with your name. You can then type in whatever response you would like as I've done in this example.

If you are looking at comments using the Revisions pane, then to reply to a comment, you need to right-click on the comment and choose Reply to Comment from the dropdown menu.

The Revisions pane option will not show the relationship between the two comments the same way that viewing them via Simple Markup or All Markup on the right-hand side of the page does. The reply is just listed like a normal comment.

So if you have a conversation that is occurring via comments, I'd recommend using Simple Markup or All Markup.

Your other option for responding to a comment is to resolve it. On the right-hand side you can click on Resolve. In the Revisions pane you can right-click and choose Resolve Comment.

When you resolve a comment, on the right-hand side that comment will be grayed-out. In the Revisions pane there's really not a noticeable difference, but the highlight of the word the comment is linked to in the document will be a lighter shade of pink.

So again, the Simple Markup or All Markup view is the better view to use in this case.

If a comment has been marked as resolved, you can reopen it.

To move between comments, use the Previous and Next options in the Comments section of the Review tab.

If a document is set to All Markup and Show All Revisions Inline then comments will appear as a set of initials and a number in brackets within the text of the document, like [MLH1]. You can hold your cursor over those initials to see the comment.

If you don't see comments in your document, but think there should be comments, use the Previous or Next option in the Comments section and they will appear.

I generally review comments in connection with track changes. If you do that, then use the Previous and Next options in the Changes section of the Review tab instead of the Previous and Next options in the Comments section because this will allow you to walk through all changes as well as all comments.

Also, since comments are treated separately from track changes, accepting all changes or rejecting all changes in a document and then turning off track changes *will not* remove the comments from the document. You must do that separately.

To remove comments, go to the Comments section of the Review tab and under the Delete option choose Delete All Comments In Document to delete all of the comments in the document.

You can also use the dropdown to delete a single comment by clicking on that comment and choosing Delete from the dropdown instead.

Deleted comments are not reflected in track changes, so be careful when deleting comments that that choice is appropriate. Marking a comment as resolved may be better until the entire team has finished their review.

Just like with track changes, if you used comments in your document at any point it is always a best practice to check that all comments have been deleted before finalizing the document.

Multilevel Lists

Multilevel lists let you construct a custom outline format for use in your document. In school we were always told to outline with I, II, III as the first level, A, B, C as the second level, 1, 2, 3 as the third level, and a, b, c as the fourth level of an outline.

I have also worked for at least one employer who took this even a step further and mandated not just a specific order of how points and subpoints were to be numbered, but also specified by exactly how much each level needed to be indented on the page.

For that employer, most employees tried to use the standard numbered list option and it didn't work. So every single report we ever prepared someone (me) had to go through the report and "fix" it. The way to fix it was to create a customized multilevel list and then apply it throughout the document.

This could have changed in recent versions of Word, but I will say that having your custom multilevel list in place in a blank document before you ever begin is the best way to work with these lists.

I highly recommend that you create at least one example of each level you need before you ever type any other word in your document because trying to to do so after the fact is...a challenge.

So how do you create a multilevel list?

The easiest option is to use one of the pre-formatted choices that Word provides. None of them are exactly what I've needed in the past, but they can at least get close to what you need and if you're not as particular as my former employers or teachers, then using one of the existing lists is the simplest way to approach things.

I count seven possible choices. To see them, go to the Paragraph section of the Home tab and click on the dropdown for Multilevel List. You will get this:

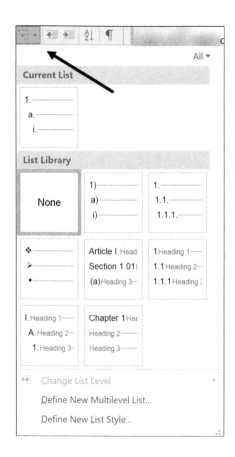

The closest one to what I described before looks like this when used:

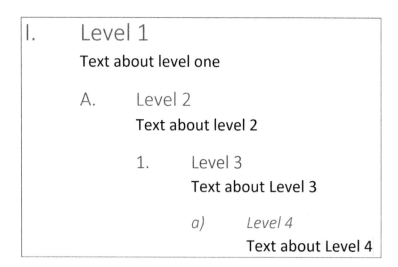

That almost works for me. I'd want to change the a with a paren for the last level to an a with a period. But the rest of it works, even those indents which are each an extra .5" per level.

Now one thing to note here with multilevel lists is that they are structured to allow text below each level.

See above where I have "Text about level..." under each of the numbered levels? I didn't have to remove a numbered value to do that. That's the default for how it works with a multilevel list (which is different from how it works with a bulleted or numbered list.) You have a numbered level, hit enter, and the next line is NOT numbered automatically when using a multilevel list.

So to get what you see above...

I went into my document, clicked on multilevel list and selected the list I wanted.

I then typed in the text for that level ("Level 1" for the first one) and hit enter.

The cursor for the next line started all the way back at the far left side of the page. To line that text up under Level 1 instead, I used tab and then typed my text ("Text about level one") and hit enter again.

At that point because I wanted another numbered level, I went back to the multilevel list dropdown menu and clicked on my list style that I had already chosen from the Current List section.

(Be careful that you don't end up running two separate lists within the same document. You can, but it may cause you lots of grief trying to keep numbering throughout your document consistent.)

Since I'd indented the line above, Word inserted an indented numbered list item that started with A. for me automatically.

I repeated the same process of adding text, enter, tab to indent, add more text, enter, and then add next list level until I had what you see above.

To change the level of a numbered line (so a line that's numbered II becomes an A or a 1 becomes a B) use the tab or shift + tab keys. You need to click onto the document right at the beginning of the text on that line (so right before the word Level in this example) and then tab will increases the indent one level, shift + tab will decrease the indent one level.

Word does not enforce any sort of hierarchical integrity. Meaning you can go from I to the next line being a) and skip right over A and 1 and Word won't do anything to warn you or prevent that. So if you're using an outline in a large document, you need to pay attention to where you are in your outline.

One way to do that is to use the Headings view in the Navigation pane. (Use Ctrl + F for find is an easy way to make it appear if it isn't already visible.) Because the other thing about the default multilevel lists is they also want to assign a heading style to each entry. (Which also means that another way to assign a level to a line within your document once you've started using a multilevel list is to assign that heading level style to that line.)

Okay. That was basic multilevel lists. Here's the ugly part: Changing one of those levels to what you want.

This is something I always struggle to get right because for some reason it always breaks some other part of my document.

For example, I mentioned above that I want that fourth level to use a period instead of a paren. You'd think you could just go in and change that one little line to be what you want and it would work. But I personally have never been able to get that to work for me. It's like squeezing a balloon. I get one part of it working and something else squishes out of shape on me.

So what I do is use the Define New Multilevel List option instead. Clicking on that option brings up the Define New Multilevel List dialogue box.

Choose each level by clicking on the number for the level on the top left.

Next, select the numbering style you want from the second dropdown menu in the number format section (I, II, III, or A, B, C, etc.).

Once you have your numbering style you can go right above that and change the format for that number to use a paren or period or whatever you want.

To do this, click into the box and add or delete what you need.

As you make these changes, the preview section in the top of the dialogue box will change to show your edits so you have an idea what the document will look like with the changes you've made.

So in the image above I've created a numbered list where it goes I, A, 1, a, i with periods first and then parens second and you can see that in the preview section.

Next, click on More in the bottom left corner and make sure that your changes are going to be applied to your whole document. (As I said before, you can have multiple lists in a document but it's problematic to do so.)

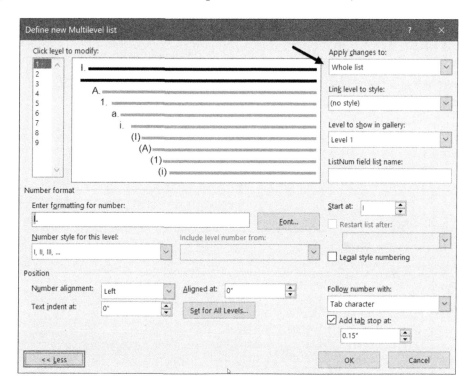

Word's help suggests that you give the list a name in the ListNum Field List Name field on the right-hand side of the top section as well and that if you want your list to use an existing style from your document you can change the Link Level to Style dropdown choice to select that style.

For every level except for the first level, make sure that the Restart List After option is checked and that the name of the prior level is showing in that dropdown box. That way if you had a point 1 with three subpoints and you're now on point 2 and it also has a subpoint that subpoint will be numbered a and not d.

The next step is to set your indents for your text and your numbers.

Let's use that employer I had who wanted a .5" indent on everything. To set that indent properly requires changing three values for each level. The Text Indent value is for how much the second line of text will be indented. The Aligned At value is for where the numbered value itself will be indented. And the Add Tab Stop At checkbox and value lets you set where the first line of text starts.

So here's what the settings would need to be for the third line of my list in order to get that result you see in the preview up top:

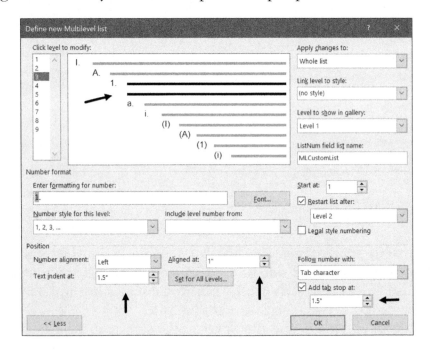

And...Going through all of that to create a custom list works. With one slight flaw.

Which is that it is no longer built to assume that if you hit enter after any numbered line that you will want text instead of another numbered entry. It acts like a numbered or bulleted list and provides the next number by default.

But to get the right spacing and formatting, that is a trade-off I'm willing to make.

One other quick point about this whole custom list process. A few times when I was creating my custom multilevel list I hit enter and it closed out the dialogue box on me even though I wasn't done.

The nice thing is that you can bring up the box again by choosing Define New Multilevel List from that dropdown and your settings will still be there. You do not have to start over if you do accidentally close the dialogue box too soon..

Ultimately, with all those settings here's what I ended up with:

```
I.      Introduction

        Some introductory text before we get started

        A.      Point 1
                1.      Subpoint 1
                        a.      Sub-Subpoint 1
                                Explanation of sub-subpoint 1 in far more detail.
                2.      Subpoint 2
                        a.      Sub-Subpoint 1
                        b.      Sub-Subpoint 1
        B.      Point 2
                1.      Subpoint 1
                2.      Subpoint 2
```

If I were using this in a real document, I would try to get in my list structure first before I went back and added the text under each point like I have here under Introduction and the first Sub-Subpoint 1.

This was not easy to build. If there is any way to use one of the defaults, do that. And if you're a fancy company that insists on your own custom list numbering and format, save yourself hundreds of thousands of dollars a year and find a way to build it once and then deploy it to all your employees as a template.

Conclusion

That's it. That's all we're going to cover in this guide.

There are other things you can do in Word. Like mail merges and adding page borders or changing your page color or adding text effects.

Mail merge generally requires understanding some Excel as well, so I covered that in a separate title called *Mail Merge for Beginners*. The others I just mentioned aren't likely to come up in a standard corporate or school setting. They could, but they haven't for me in thirty years and my goal with these guides was to keep the amount I covered to a manageable level.

But now that we're at the end, I hope you can see that Word (and Excel and PowerPoint and Access and even Outlook as well) follow a certain logic. Once you start to understand that logic it's pretty easy to know what should or should not be doable in any given program and to go find the steps to do it if it is a possibility.

Word's Help is excellent. There were a few times writing this book that I used it to confirm something or to verify that a specific task worked in a specific way.

To access it, you can click on the Help tab and then Help again. That will bring up the Help task pane where you can search for what you need to know.

For some tasks, like the Format Painter in the Clipboard section of the Home tab, you can also hold your mouse over the option and see a Tell Me More link. Click on that and it will open the Help task pane to a page specific to that task.

If that doesn't work, because maybe you need to know how to do something specific, there are a number of internet user forums where people discuss how to perform various tasks in Word and also a number of blogs where people have posted about how to perform various tasks. A quick internet search on what you're trying to do, "mail merge Word 2019" for example, should bring up a number of results.

You can also post a question in a user forum, but beware that you may receive a few snide comments back if you don't provide a very clear question that explains exactly what you need to do and what version of the program you're using.

If you do find an answer on a forum or a blog, be careful. Don't click on links posted by random strangers on the internet. That's a good way to get a virus.

And don't give someone you don't trust remote access to your computer. Or open a file they send you. Basically, don't be too trusting.

You can also email me at mlhumphreywriter@gmail.com.

I can't guarantee I'll be able to answer every single question, but I can probably handle most of them and I'm happy to help.

So there you have it. I hope this book was helpful and best of luck.

INDEX

CONTROL SHORTCUTS

The following is a list of useful control shortcuts in Word. For each one, hold down the Ctrl key and use the listed letter to perform the command.

Command	Ctrl +
Center Text	E
Copy	C
Cut	X
Find	F
Go To	G
Insert Link	K
Page Break	Enter
Paste	V
Print	P
Redo	Y
Replace	H
Save	S
Select All	A
Undo	Z

ABOUT THE AUTHOR

M.L. Humphrey is a former stockbroker with a degree in Economics from Stanford and an MBA from Wharton who has spent close to twenty years as a regulator and consultant in the financial services industry.

You can reach M.L. Humphrey at:

mlhumphreywriter@gmail.com

or at

www.mlhumphrey.com